PRAISE FOR
BEEP! BEEP! GET OUT OF MY WAY!

"In a pond filled with self-help books, Catherine DeMonte's *Beep! Beep! Get Out of my Way!* will be the very last frog you'll need to kiss to finally get the royal, plentiful life you so desire. Her acute insight, loving compassion, honest openness, and practical tools will guide your journey, as it has mine, to receive the abundance and fulfillment you've longed for, as you reach a deeper, joyful understanding of your own unique and sacred path. Her Abundance Circle practice -shared in this book, provides you with the mental and spiritual equipment you need to jumpstart the motor of your passion and awareness, allowing what is meant to be yours manifest in your life for once and for all. Be prepared to become, like she tells us, a 'Rock Star Superpower Badass Creator'!"

—Iran Daniel, Emmy Winner, Actor, Writer, Producer @irandaniel

"Save yourself years of therapy- this book cuts to the chase and is incredibly useful. *Beep! Beep!* crunches heady, abstract concepts into practical, easy to read steps.

The steps Catherine lays out for looking inward, overcoming personal obstacles and getting what you want is straightforward and do-able. Her writing style is the best blend of practical insights, sharing vulnerably and why we want to look inward.

Her book is like having coffee with your best friend, if your best friend was Yoda. Or Oprah."

—Tally Barr, TV Executive Producer

"Catherine DeMonte's *Beep! Beep! Get Out of My Way!* is smart, insightful and inspiring. It's for every person who's had a 'I can't take it anymore!'

moment and is ready to manifest their heart's deepest desires. Catherine takes the reader on a journey of self-discovery to identify what has been getting in their way and leads them by the hand to walk a new path to receive exactly what they want, and more! Catherine's writing is thought-provoking, heartfelt and sincere. Her grace and gratitude shine through on every page. *Beep! Beep! Get Out of My Way!* is a must-read for everyone who has a desire that they haven't been able to fulfill."

—Tabby Biddle, Author of
Find Your Voice: A Woman's Call to Action and TEDx Speaker

"My soul was enriched and encouraged as I read this book. The writing is so personal and real-- and it even took me on a soulfully-spiritual journey! Catherine's compassionate touch and her courage to dig deep into the patterns of her own life really helped me not feel so alone or ashamed of my journey.

Beep! Beep! has shown me how I've been playing small in some areas and that evolution and abundance are my birthright! Catherine has affirmed that I'm just a tool away from a radically different life and the book creatively and uniquely invited me on a journey to heal and rise strong. I'm grateful for the manifestation of a new way!

The principles are practical yet thought-provoking; they help guide me in doing inner work.

This book has helped me reflect on some of the fear-based choices that I've been making-- I have a deeper awareness of how to make healthy "love-based" choices intentionally. I'm grateful!"

—Michael McGill, Jr., Motivational Speaker and Author of
Soul Vitamins: Minerals for the Mind, Body and Soul
Mcgillspeaks.com

"Catherine's book will inspire and heal you by helping you explore - as she does in her groups - what might be blocking you from receiving what you desire, in the most loving, compassionate and thoughtful way. I found it inspiring, relatable and very healing. I highly recommend her work to clients and to friends."

—Anna Stookey, Psychotherapist
Bodymindguide.com

"This book captures Catherine DeMonte's compassion, enthusiasm and positivity. Her methodology is illustrated with rich personal anecdotes and inspiring examples from those who have already benefited from her teachings through her Abundance Circles."

—Sonia Greaven, Ph.D., Calabasas Clinical Psychologist

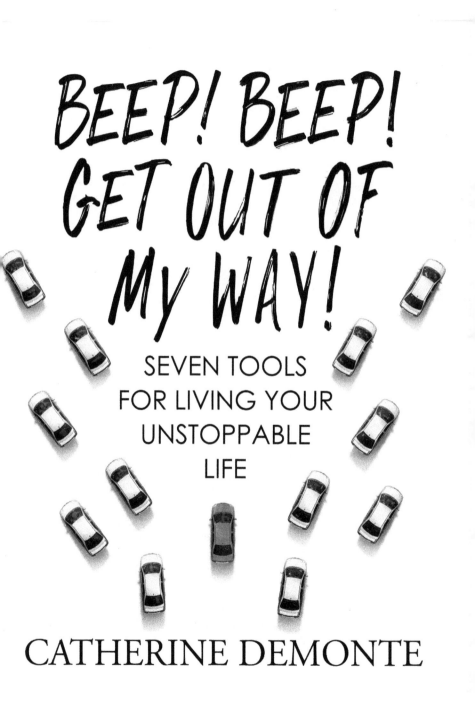

BEEP! BEEP! GET OUT OF MY WAY!

SEVEN TOOLS FOR LIVING YOUR UNSTOPPABLE LIFE

CATHERINE DEMONTE

For my beloved, Tim. You are my rock.
Thank you for your undying faith, love, and support.

For my sons Jacob and Gabriel.
You hang the stars and the moon in my sky. You are my "Sonlight."

CONTENTS

Introduction 1

Chapter 1 15
Wounds: How the Light Gets In 15

Chapter 2 26
Tool 1: Deep Desire + Work in Theory 26

Chapter 3 35
Tool 1: Deep Desire + Work in Practice 35

Chapter 4 59
Tool 2: The Finesse of Receiving 59

Chapter 5 77
Tool 3: Shadow Material 77

Chapter 6 94
Tool 4: "I AM" Statements 94

Chapter 7 105
Tool 5: Love Versus Fear 105

Chapter 8 124
Tool 6: The Magic of Synchronicity.. 124

Chapter 9 140
Tool 7: Grace and Gratitude.. 140

Chapter 10..152
Wrapping It All Up in a Sheer Silk Ribbon............................ 152

Acknowledgments 163

About the Author 165

INTRODUCTION

A<small>S A PSYCHOTHERAPIST IN PRIVATE</small> practice for more than twenty-five years, I have long had the privilege of working with incredibly wonderful people seeking to become their best and highest selves as they endeavor to make their lives more satisfying and fulfilling. It's an honor to witness my clients bravely face the issues and roadblocks in their lives as they dedicate themselves to their own healing and profound growth. It's a cherished gift to see the positive transformation psychotherapy has created in people that I come to care so deeply about.

We usually discover that tending to "the thing" that brought them in to see me in the first place—the affair, painful childhood memories, the feeling of utter brokenness, the death of a loved one, their reactive parenting style, whatever it is—turns out to be their greatest teacher. We could call the lessons gleaned from these rough life experiences "the gifts wrapped in sandpaper," as author Lisa Nichols says. Without them, we don't pay attention to places that need tending. And without tending to those wounds, limiting self-judgment, and silencing critical inner voices, it is difficult—if not impossible—to lead the kind of life we want and deserve.

It's also impossible to attract the thing you most deeply desire.

Like me—like all of us—you have been trying to manifest, or call in, something that has been elusive. Maybe just the one "big" thing: more money, a life partner, or a desire to bring your work to a bigger stage and reach more people. Maybe you manifest smaller things often and with ease. Parking lot spaces, for instance! Every. Single. Time. So perhaps you have asked yourself, "Then why not the 'Big One' my heart deeply desires and that my life feels incomplete without? Why can I manifest the perfect spot to park my car in a full lot the very moment I remember to ask for it, but have been waiting for financial abundance (or a life partner or my ship to come in) all this bloody time?"

Would it surprise you to learn that there is a reason the "Big One" gets away?

There are blocks to manifesting the life of our dreams, and a lot of visualizing and stating affirmations alone won't call it in. I know because my own Big One eluded me for *decades.* Perhaps yours has too, or you are worried it will. Yes and yes?

First, you need to understand the unconscious belief system that runs your own personal metaphoric manifestation bus. Then you need to know and use the seven tools I discuss in this book that will bring your deeply desired object from your mind and into your life. Some of these tools you may recognize, or possibly have used before. It's using them together, in the order they appear in this book, and removing the blocks your desires run into, that will allow what you desire to show up.

So first of all, my friend, what's your story?

LOOKING AT YOUR STORY

TIM IS THE MIDDLE OF six children. A typical middle child, he was self-sufficient, adaptable, and a good listener. He was quieter than his older siblings and a good older brother to the younger ones, whom he remembers picking up and holding as if they were dolls or puppies.

He was resourceful. He and his next-older brother had paper routes in school for many years to make some money of their own.

With his beard and soft eyes, people often told him that he looked like Dan Fogelberg or Kenny Loggins, two folk-rock singers of that time. He was tri-captain of the football team at his private East Coast Catholic high school and ranked among the top ten wrestlers in the state of Connecticut.

Tim and his mom were very close and shared a tight bond, especially during his last two years of high school and first year of college. He was still living at home that year of college and they often sat together at the table in the kitchen and talked at length. Sometimes she asked for his input on things, and sometimes they spoke about ethics, books, or current events. They shared interests and had the same warm, calm demeanor.

When he was twenty-one, his mother drove alone one November afternoon to the naval air station about forty miles from their home to buy less expensive groceries for the Thanksgiving dinner she'd be cooking for their large family. On the way there, she fell asleep at the wheel on the quiet country highway outside of town, drove into a ditch, and crashed. She was hurt badly. Her body slammed into the steering wheel. She broke several ribs and her wrist and sustained a lot of internal damage.

Fortunately, a passing driver found her car and she was taken to a hospital. This was in 1979, a time well before cell phones, and it was miraculous that she got help. Because of her many internal injuries, she was placed in the Intensive Care Unit. After a couple of days, she appeared to be strong enough to be taken out of the ICU and placed in a regular hospital room, but she was still in a lot of pain from the accident. Her internal injuries were more severe than previously thought and she'd been released from ICU too early. The doctors discovered more injuries and internal bleeding, so they took her in to operate. She did not make it through the surgery and died on the operating table about six days after her accident.

Aileen was a devoted and dedicated mother and deeply religious. She was the heart and center of the home and, with her passing, the family unraveled. Tim's father, a good man but overwhelmed and in deep grief himself, detached from the family. In a short time, he sold the family home and married, in a private ceremony, a divorced woman he knew before Aileen died. His children learned of the marriage after the fact. The newly married couple got their own place. With his new life quickly settling in after the death of his wife, he became increasingly remote and uninvolved in his children's lives. The children were motherless and rudderless. Tim's younger sister got married at eighteen and moved to another state, and his two older brothers had moved out of town to go to school. Tim and his two younger siblings needed a house.

At twenty-two, Tim hit adulthood running. He put college on hold, worked full time, and bought a house. His two younger brothers moved with him and, leveraging all angles to keep income flowing, he added renters, two strangers who each rented a bedroom. Now there were five guys in the house, each living a life disconnected from the others. Tim worked two jobs: installing fire control systems in restaurants on the weekdays, and at a dam-building project eighty miles away on the weekends. He worked long hours, often seven days a week, and was rarely at the house because of it, so he and his two younger, high school-aged brothers were all in their own orbits. The house wasn't a place where the brothers gathered together for dinner at night to catch up with each other's news or enjoyed sitting around playing cards together. It was more like "every man for himself" in a shared space.

Although Tim worked nonstop, money was always tight. It was hard to suddenly have large "adult" financial responsibilities like making mortgage payments. It was also hard to earn much money without a college degree or job training, other than what he was learning on the jobs he had at the time. Hard too to make that little bit of money stretch for himself and the household he was now responsible for.

So, Tim's money story—and we all have one—is that you have to work very, very hard and yet feel constantly in a state of responsibility, overwhelmed with a staggering sense of there never being enough money despite the long hours of work. Money will still be tight. Tim had the worst of both worlds. It's one thing to work very hard but make enough to pay for a nice house, cover your bills, and fund vacations, travel, and fun *or* to work fewer hours and possibly make less money but have time to be with family or do the things you love to do. It's another to work hard and still never have enough.

Tim is a generous, smart, resourceful, unselfish, admirable human being. What he did for his brothers and family was with pure heart; an act of love. But he was young and struggling, with no guidance. His plans to finish college were suddenly severed and he was propelled into a drastic story: "You have to work very long and very hard, but there will still never be enough." This was the story he found himself living in after the sudden trauma of losing his mother. He didn't know there was any truth or choice other than the financial story he was living in.

Tim is my husband.

My money story is this: I arrived in the world to my mother, father, and a three-year-old sister. Adding to the family was a conscious decision and my parents planned their pregnancy. But what they did *not* plan for was having twins. In fact, my parents didn't know my mother was pregnant with twins until after my sister Becky was born, nine minutes before me, and my mother could feel me still inside her womb. She told the delivering doctor there was "still another one." The nurse on duty put her hand on my mother's belly and could feel that there was indeed another baby inside.

According to my mother, who told this story often, the doctor scoffed in a condescending way at both women until the nurse insisted my mom was right. That's why there was a long nine minutes between Becky's birth and mine.

Growing up a twin, or "womb-mate," as we like to say, was fun, like having a built-in best friend. However, it also meant hearing how difficult and *expensive* it was to suddenly have two babies instead of one. Not only did my parents now need two of everything— two cribs, two sets of clothes and diapers, two bottles, two sets of toys—it also meant deeper exhaustion for my parents. I often heard how my mom would put one of us in the crib only to have the other, already sleeping baby wake up and cry and wake up the newly sleeping one, and how that meant it was hard to get a break.

As we grew, our older sister went to camp during summer vacations twice, but we never did. We were told it was because our parents couldn't afford to send two of us. Our older sister was given some other things we were not with the same explanation. It didn't seem harsh; it seemed practical. Just a fact.

We arrived early and tiny, so we had to stay behind in the hospital for a couple of weeks after the delivery, which disrupts the bonding and attachment between a mother and her baby. Our mother did not nurse us as she had her first, either because we remained in the hospital, causing her milk to dry, or because there were two of us, both which were the reasons she gave me when I asked over the years. Having more children than expected and then a forced separation could not have been good for bonding.

I heard stories about how emotionally, physically, and financially difficult that period was on my mother. Although they were not told in a harsh or blaming tone, it was clear that having unexpected twins was difficult and burdensome, which I can intellectually understand.

My money story was that I was unexpected and there wasn't enough money to accommodate me. Although it was never intended to "land" that way inside of my childhood mind, it's what I took on as truth. My parents were lovely, caring, demonstrative people who loved us all dearly and whom I loved right back. It's the meaning *I* attached to what I heard that made me believe, "There isn't enough for me and I shouldn't want more." Because I was a kind of unexpected guest, I think my birth story made me push down my needs and expectations. With much adult reflection, I have learned that I took on the belief that it was a lot of work and expense to have me arrive the way I did and I should squash my material desires. I got my first job while still in junior high school. When I wanted extra things, I used money I earned myself from babysitting to buy them, and I purposefully tried to not ask for things. Well into my early adulthood, I struggled financially and went without because money was always tight.

This was in the 1980s, long before wealth consciousness was as well understood, and two decades before *The Secret* came out, a time when stoicism was not only the norm but also kind of revered. So I didn't know about limiting money beliefs, and I wouldn't have complained if I did.

There's a therapist's expression that says, "His claws fit her wounds" (or vice versa). You can see that Tim's money story of having to work really hard but never having enough fits my story of not having enough but "being okay" going without. Our shared story recreated both of our stories of financial struggle. So for much of our married life, Tim and I went on like this, with him being away at work seven days a week and working evenings at home as his early money programming had taught him to do, but things always feeling extremely tight financially. I always wanted to see him more, travel together, and do more things, even free things like taking walks or going to the beach together, but he was always working.

I bought into Tim's money story of not having enough because it fit my own money story. I didn't have the awareness then to question it: It was programming that ran under my conscious radar. I didn't know then that what you unconsciously believe to be true is what you get. All I knew was that money was always tight and that I rarely did things with my husband. What I didn't know was how to ask for what I needed to receive.

It's pretty ridiculous how our stories feel true and acceptable as fact and drive our life's metaphoric bus. I got married at twenty-three. I had the notion that all young couples struggle financially. Then I thought all college and post-graduate students did. When our first son was born, I thought all young parents did. And so it went. I lived in a state of "When, then," meaning I carried a belief that when a certain thing happened or a certain phase was over, then money would be more plentiful. Besides, we were young and in love; what difference did it make if money was tight?

Discontentment grew. Tim continued to try and pedal faster and work harder to provide and move forward and spent little time at home as a result, which continued to feed into my story that there was not enough. Not enough time together, not enough connection, and not enough money.

I was emotionally stuffing my desire for more connection and time together and did so for many years, not realizing I had the power to rewrite the story or make another choice. Part of the stuffing was because it felt situational. I was in graduate school full-time, which was expensive for us, and I had an unpaid, full-time internship in order to earn hours toward my therapist's license.

I was also grateful for Tim's working hard and didn't want to be ungrateful. "Providing" is a love language, after all.

Our financial story and the reality of scarcity we created around it meant we would sometimes be strapped to make payments on the larger-cost items like the mortgage, cars, and our taxes, which got us behind and created debt. To further our belief that there was enough, if the topic of travel or anything "unnecessary" came up, we could realistically respond, "It would be irresponsible to do that now. If we had money for that, we should put it towards our debt. But *when* there's enough, we can do those fun things!"

If, when.

The Law of Attraction says that even stating "there is not enough" like we were was creating exactly that. Not enough.

It's one thing to understand something intellectually. But our heart's message pulls us in a different direction and says it can be different from the way it's been. Something else can be better and more aligned with our truth. Living in a situation and believing it to be the unwanted "normal" deepens the groove that it is the only truth.

Looking over the top of that supposed truth and into the expanse of the sky above can lead to a new reality.

Tim and I lived together in the land of "not enoughness" because each of us believed the separate money stories of our childhoods, which then fit together like a glove slipping easily onto a hand. We lived under the hypnosis of that interactive story for over twenty years, dragging it behind us through early marriage, grad school, and early parenthood. Twenty-plus years of financial stressing, struggling, stuffing, and thinking the only remedy was more of the same: Just keep working and going without doing the things you really want to do, like travel.

It wasn't just a lack of money to do what we wanted to do, but also strife about getting into debt and not having much in savings. It was like having an invisible anvil hanging over our heads, ready to drop at any time, for years. Perhaps you know this feeling too. Maybe your anvil isn't about money, but about not having a partner and feeling lonely. Or not being able to conceive a baby. Or not doing the work you know you are here to do. Whatever it is for you, I know you get what I am talking about when I say that living in a state of not having it feels soul-crushing and paralyzing. When your life is pretty good except one big thing feels missing or you feel stuck, for years, the ache of going without seems to settle in your bones.

I understand your pain and get it because I struggled with my own pain unnecessarily for too long myself. Then I got out of it and taught my clients to as well. When you change your story—and your *life*—there is no going back to the old way. Never, ever, ever.

It's so much nicer in the flow.

* * *

So THEN CAME THE BIG Shift. Here is how it happened: Around twenty-five years into my therapy private practice, the concept of Abundance Circles came to me. It wasn't necessarily a gentle, easy arrival, like your best friend showing up at your birthday party. Rather, it was born out of a moment of my own frustration and pain.

My husband and I were both working hard, doing the best we could, but money still felt extremely tight. And it wasn't good for the marriage for us to focus on keeping ourselves afloat more than we focused on our relationship. We saw each other in the evenings for dinner, rarely on weekend days when Tim was working, and almost never for excursions away. Although it was and is a warm relationship with a lot of love, this is not a good formula for conscious connection.

We put traveling and vacations off, mostly because of other life choices such as attempting to pay off our debts, living in high-cost Los Angeles, and choosing a private school for our sons instead of local public schools because we felt equally passionate about the school as we did about travel. And with Tim now in real estate, he wanted to be consistently available to his clients on the weekends. All this made even short, inexpensive weekend trips seem impossible at the time.

Meanwhile, it seemed like other people were constantly taking amazing trips or going off on weekend getaways. I would feel happy for them, but sad for us. And over the years, social media amplified that; we live in an age when we can peek into people's lives in a way that was unavailable to us before on this large scale. And so it seemed that everyone was traveling or doing things with their partners or families. All the time. The bottom line was that I wasn't making it happen.

Then one day, I heard yet another story of someone going someplace wonderful and I hit a breaking point. I let out a low groan and said, "Ugh, I can't take it anymore!" It wasn't just not traveling. It was the frustration of money feeling tight and the oppression of debt. It was the worry, at times, that we could lose the house. Others' travel was just the visible reminder. "Not having enough" was the real issue.

When I allowed myself to feel the frustration, to be completely fed up instead of considering our state "situational" and being understanding, something happened. I shifted immediately. I could no longer *not* have the life I imagined for myself.

That's when the tools that make up the eight-session, small-group Abundance Circle groups I hold as part of my private psychotherapy practice came to me. They came easily over the course of a week, almost like a download or as if channeled. These tools proved to be life-changing for the Abundance Circle participants. They became the catalyst for the book you are holding. They can be life-changing for you as well.

The seven manifesting tools just came into my awareness—one by one, in the order you will find them here, and in a sequence that makes perfect sense. I would see something in my life frequently for some time; I'd see the concept everywhere until it soaked in that it was the next tool. For example, for the tool *Receiving*, I'd see or hear mention of the word *receiving* everywhere. I saw the word on a license plate and read about the importance of being able to receive in an email someone sent, then an article, and then a friend would tell me she is trying to be better about receiving and why.

Then *Shadow Material*—I'd see *that* phrase everywhere. It was as if I was having a sacred dialogue with the Universe. "This is about an Abundance Circle," I'd think. "These are tools for helping myself and others manifest what we want in life."

I applied the tools in my own life and experienced a massive shift, both internal and external. Work with my clients went to deeper levels in a short time. Insights about what would be helpful for them to know came to me with distinct clarity, and my clients were having breakthroughs and deep insights that were profoundly healing and rewarding. I was also receiving more new clients all the time. My private therapy practice was the fullest it had ever been, and the work more effective. Despite being busier than ever, I felt more energized than before because I was so jazzed about the shifts going on for and around me.

I began sharing concepts of some of the individual tools with clients randomly, as I saw fit, during our sessions, and saw big shifts quickly. Then I realized that if I shared all the tools, in the order they came into my awareness, and in a group instead of just in individual client sessions, it would be exponentially more powerful. It is incentivizing to speak our desires out loud. It keeps us accountable. And our words are "made real" in the world when spoken to others. It's also supportive of us to have our visions held up by others, just as it is for others when we hold up theirs. This mirroring process is profound.

In groups, it's as if we are, in a sense, saying to each other, "I see your desires and I raise you one," to whatever the person desires to create or manifest. A supportive "other" hearing and then holding our deepest desires for us makes us become even more steadfast in wanting to make that desire a reality. It raises our commitment to bringing it to life. Having them see it, *maybe something even bigger than we originally had in mind,* and sometimes offer ideas about getting there that we haven't even thought of ourselves, lights our fire.

However, even if you are not in one of the Abundance Circles, you can get the benefit of the practice by learning about these abundance-magnifying tools and doing the exercises in this book by yourself or with a partner.

If you had a way of amplifying your own desires exponentially, so that your voice was stronger and clearer and therefore better heard by the Universe and you could receive what you are deeply longing for even if you aren't in an Abundance Circle yourself, would you give that to yourself? I imagine you would. In fact, you do have a way: You are holding it. This book shows you how to create that amplification in your own life because all of the Abundance Circle tools are in it.

Imagine a planet of people who all felt satisfied, content, and joyous. This would be a very different place. Digging deep into your desires and stopping at nothing to fulfill them, including looking at blocks and the not-always-comfortable Shadow material that prevents us from fully showing up, is actually your life's mandate. Therefore, it's not good when you don't fully show up—not only for you, but for the planet that is waiting for your magnificent, beautiful, shining self and all the gifts you are meant to bring.

The Universe cannot evolve any further until *you* evolve further. How much support is there for your evolution? That support is infinite and available at all times. Who is relying on you? Everyone. This is not meant to intimidate you. It's meant to invite you. This is your gold-embossed invitation, handed to you on a beautiful tray by a devoted, loyal friend, requesting that you please bring out the gifts you have been burying or do the things you haven't done yet because old fears, wounds, or "stories" prevented it from showing up for you.

These seven tools will turn your fear-based choices to love-filled choices, your wounds into your strengths, and your stories into your truth.

Each of the seven tools is mighty powerful alone, but combined? Whoo-eee! You're going to be a Rock Star Superpower Badass Creator! That is a lot to put on your superhero chest, so maybe you could just write "R.S.S.B.C." The abbreviation won't matter.

Everyone will know who you are anyway.

CHAPTER 1
WOUNDS: HOW THE LIGHT GETS IN

One day, in retrospect, the years of struggle
will strike you as the most beautiful.

—Sigmund Freud

DESIRING MORE MONEY IN YOUR life is not greedy. Desiring to play on a bigger stage is not vanity. Desiring love and a relationship in your life is not selfishness. And desire to express your gifts in the world is not egotistical. These are in fact the things you came into the world to receive and to express. They are your soul's mandates. Who are you *not* to have and be these things, when having and being them makes you happier, less stressed, and able to contribute more to the world?

If someone who loved you gifted you an expensive, beautiful diamond ring, would you stuff it in a box in your sock drawer because you were afraid of what others would think if they saw it on your finger? Or would you wear it where you could appreciate its shining brilliance and exquisite beauty, reminding you of that person's generosity and love for you?

How could hiding the gifts you've been given ever serve you?

Having more money allows you to do more good in the world. You can contribute to charities and causes that you are passionate about. You can provide for others who are in need. You can live a less financially restrictive life, freeing yourself from constrictive worry and thoughts of there not being enough, which allows for expansion of self in other ways. The opening of financial freedom and abundance creates opportunities that aren't there when money is tight.

The same is true for playing larger in your life or having a relationship. When you feel expansive and are utilizing your gifts, or you're in a relationship, if that is what you choose, you have more life-giving energy in your reservoir. You feel less stress and more joy. When your heart swells with love, you're a robust version of yourself. You're more "lit up." You're living a life on fire. There is more of you to give, more for others, more for yourself, and more for the world.

So, given all that, why wouldn't we all be living life as our best selves; feeling content, loving deeply, being at peace, and never playing small? If the aforementioned qualities are good things and feel good, why don't we just stay there? Psychologists would tell us the answer to this rests on three small, one-syllable words:

We get hurt.

The hurts could be emotional or physical, intentionally inflicted or circumstantial, or have nothing whatsoever to do with us. It doesn't matter. We are little balls of needs as children and are wholly dependent on another to meet those needs. If those needs were not met, it created scary feelings for us, and rightfully so. Babies and children cannot survive without adults seeing to their needs. We need to be fed, picked up, touched, loved, have our diaper changed, kept warm, and kept out of harm's way. We need sleep; we need peace; we need attention.

Along the way, sometimes, some of those needs don't get met. That happens even with the best of parenting and may sometimes be unintentional or unavoidable. Babies and children are sponges and soak up the energy around them as they try to make sense of this place they are in. Much of what they absorb isn't even about them, but the fact of the absorption is inevitable. There is no escaping it. It's just how we're designed. Not all our developmental needs will be met in every circumstance. And sometimes bad things happen to children.

Such experiences leave marks that we register as trauma and tell us to beware of them happening again. We tell ourselves stories about these events. We might make up the story that we made our daddy or mommy go away in the case of a divorce or death. We may think Mommy or Daddy's depression is because they don't like us.

Little folks often erroneously take on the responsibility for whatever they are feeling from the big folks around them. Stands to reason, right? Babies and children are healthily narcissistic. They truly believe the world revolves around them. Who else is there?! All they know is the world they see and that they are in it. You have only to observe an infant crying for milk "Now!" at 2:00 a.m. or a three-year-old not wanting to share her toy to recognize that.

Meeting those narcissistic, so-called "self-centered" needs for an infant creates a healthy sense of self because it creates the feeling the world is a safe place, that needs will be met. If we grow up believing our needs *won't* be met, it can result in us squashing those needs and our voice, or feeling entitled and self-centered, or craving and demanding unending attention to fill the hole inside. In other words, someone whose needs go unmet as a child may become a *narcissist*.

As we grow, more opportunities arise for needs to go unmet or for us to tell ourselves stories about the things going on around us. There are as many stories as there are people walking around on the planet. And what might create a profound core wound for one person might land differently for another or not leave a mark at all on another. Things like personality and resilience level, age, birth order, and how the adults around them handled events have an impact. All of these factors influence how what happens will affect a person.

Not all the stories we tell ourselves came from traumatic experiences. Some were positive. As an example of this, my middle-child-of-six husband recalls being about five years old when two or three cute teenage girls were over at his house, talking to him and giving him a lot of positive attention. He was sitting on the edge of a kitchen counter where they had placed him and they were standing around him, smiling at him and talking to each other about how cute he was. Tim sat there quietly grinning, taking it in.

One of the girls said, "Oh, he is so cute! He is so quiet!" The "quiet" attribute lodged in his brain as a positive thing. I don't know if this ever happened, but let's say that at some time after this positive event, Tim was playing quietly in his room or reading a book and his mother said, "Timmy, I like how nice and quiet you are being." Or he was told he was a good boy for sitting quietly in church. That comment would have a place to "land" or a "shelf," as I often call it with my therapy clients. Tim's mom's comment would land on top of the positive experience with the girls.

When positive things happen, feel-good chemicals fire in our brains and we want to keep doing more of whatever we did that elicited that feeling. Our brain cells communicate myriad feelings to each other via synaptic transmission—in simple terms, one brain cell releases a chemical reaction to a situation, and another cell absorbs it. This process is called "neuronal firing."

Frequently traveled neural pathways are more efficient. If an experience happens over and over again, like being told that being quiet is a good thing, we believe it to be true without question. After all, we have all this "proof." The thing is, we can find "proof" of whatever our belief system tells us is true. We could find proof in opposite directions. My happy childhood may tell me the world is a loving, compassionate, safe, and benevolent place, whereas someone who grew up in terrible circumstances will understandably believe it to be harsh, scary, lonely, and that people are "out to get you." Both sides could make a case for their beliefs. And neither could be called "wrong." It just depends through which lenses you see the world.

We end up making judgments very quickly based on things we see or experience and file them as fact based on what our subconscious mind tells us to be true. Our *sub*conscious mind. The subconscious mind processes about four hundred billion bits of information per second and travels up to a hundred thousand miles per hour! The *conscious* mind, on the other hand, processes only about two thousand pieces of information and travels only about one hundred miles per hour.

We end up seeking what feels like proof of our stories and attracting those stories in. Your strong belief in something draws it in or may even have you believing that it's happening when it isn't. Each of these instances then gives us more evidence to build our case. This in turns fires the neurons, which deepens the belief: now we can even "feel it in our bones" to be true.

Around and around the merry-go-round it goes, this circle of Event

To belief about ourselves because of the event,

To creating a wound or limiting story about ourselves because of the event,

To attracting the story in or seeing it where it isn't really happening,

To firing neurons to further deepen the original belief,

To creating feelings in the body that our story is true and anchoring it,

To further "proving" it to be true...

It can be anything from "All people leave me" or "I'm fat" to "Nobody cares about me," "I have to be funny to be liked," or "I am not enough." The message gets thought about and reenacted over and over again in the brain. With so much repetition, it becomes automatic. We think the belief is true because we have "practiced" it in our mind over and over again, like learning the alphabet in kindergarten.

This process was cleverly described as "Neurons that fire together, wire together," by Canadian neuropsychologist Donald Hebb in 1949. He knew that every emotion and experience we have triggers thousands of neurons that form a network of neural communication. So, when we have a similar situation pop up in our life—or one that feels similar—the brain learns to trigger the same neurons each time.

"This current thing smacks a lot of that old thing I experienced, so it must be the same," we think on a subconscious level.

A common example of this is when you have an argument with someone. You might say that when they said X, it made you irate, to which they say, "But I didn't say that! I said XYZ." And you say, "Yes you did! I know what I heard." And they say, "I know what I *said.*" Chances are you heard X through your wound. You may be convinced you heard it a certain way; even your body is aligning with you and it feels familiar. But know this: Getting triggered is a clue that a comment or experience went through your own filter.

We don't get triggered by something if we don't have a wound there.

That's why we don't all get worked up by the same things.

When I first heard about wounds, my association was that having them was not very healthy. Or they had to show up in big, dark ways like having road rage or throwing plates in an argument. I heard the term early on in my therapy studies and practice. By then, I'd already done some inner work, made a big point of *trying* to always hear another person's point of view without getting defensive, and was pretty calm and happy in life. My childhood was mostly a happy, uneventful, steady one. Therefore, when I heard the word "wounds" in the context of being triggered, I actually thought I didn't have any! "Whew. Dodged *that* bullet!"

That sounds both naïve and arrogant to even consider, now, but I didn't mean it from a feeling *evolved* place. I meant it from a feeling *lucky* place. I must have thought a relatively happy childhood meant you got out unscathed and had no unconscious stories or limiting beliefs.

That's what wounds look like. They are under the radar.

Under the radar, but driving the bus.

* * *

Forget your perfect offering.
There is a crack, a crack, in everything.
That's how the light gets in.

—Leonard Cohen

THERE IS A CENTURIES-OLD JAPANESE art form of repairing broken pottery by infusing the crack with gold, called *kintsugi*. This practice not only saves the piece from being tossed but sees the broken part as salvageable, and the value of enhancing the beauty of the "flaw" by highlighting it. The gold in the crack *illuminates* the crack. So too, the places you have struggled, the rough things you have been through, are the places you can fill in with gold.

It's when you dive deep into your own strengths and gifts and became a truer version of yourself. Our biggest burst of personal growth can happen when we bump into the hard places. It's when we, hopefully, look within to see when we felt this way before so we can begin the healing process. The current, conscious hurt or deep emotion can bring up older, unconscious hurts and be tended to by our adult self, thereby removing our reactive behavior and blocks that stop the good stuff from coming in. Digging into where our wounds originated is where the healing and growth takes place and where conscious change can begin. This creates a more authentic *you*.

Think of it like polishing a mirror. "If you are irritated by every rub, how will your mirror be polished?" asked the great Persian poet Rumi.

However, knowing this and going through the heartbreaks and breakups, the pain and the agony, are two different things. It's ideal to come from an "observe, don't judge" state in life, and to trust that "it's all good, even the rough stuff"—a phrase I created for the hard times. Ideally, we learn to be a witness to the events that surround our lives and grow from the experiences.

In a perfect world, we are so emotionally mature that when things rub us the wrong way, we are able to step back, take a breath, and ask what is there for us to learn. Yet to do so hardly seems humanly possible as our heart breaks at the atrocities and heartaches not only in our own life, but also those we see happening in the world at large. We want and *need* to retain our empathy for others. We want and *need* to have our own emotions and reactions to the events in our life and have compassion for the hurt place inside.

As a psychotherapist for more than twenty-five years, I have listened to many painful stories from people I have come to care for quite deeply: stories of infidelity, miscarriage, broken childhoods, or feeling rudderless which are hard to speak about, let alone go through. And sometimes they speak of choices I personally wouldn't make or address their children or partners in a way I wouldn't or in ways that are disruptive and harmful, and my task is to point out healthier ways to communicate. In order to offer comfort in the hard times or advice in the unkind times in their lives, I need to be able to sit without judgment as they tell me these things.

The point is, I have taught myself to observe, not judge. Meaning—and here is the good news—it's a teachable thing. We can all learn it. In my work, this not only helps me assist my clients to find the gold within themselves that will fill in their cracks, but also helps me avoid bringing other people's issues into my own being. One can have deep and profound empathy for others without absorbing their pain. I think of it as the difference between holding something for someone for a bit or actually letting it into our bodies. You can understand something is on their path and walk with them without taking that issue home with you.

I often hold my clients and their struggles inside my heart long after they walk out of my office. I send positive thoughts their way, or a thought of something might pop up between sessions that will be good to tell them about, even if it's about a better way to handle something and I sense it will make them defensive to hear it. But it must come from an "observe, not judge" place or I'd be stepping in as their own adult self.

You can do that for yourself. You can become the inner therapist or *kintsugi* artist in your own life and pull in what feels missing in your life by doing so.

* * *

HAVING DONE YEARS AND YEARS of my own inner work, I was quite conscious of my "unexpected guest" story and had come a long way in reversing it. Sometimes unraveling the old story was difficult and brought up painful memories, and sometimes it was freeing and liberating. The more inner work I did, the more I saw the positive shifts on the outside.

Yet my money story was still, apparently, that "I don't deserve" or "I am okay going without" and money was therefore always tight. I say "apparently" because despite a lot of positivity in my life, it always felt like there wasn't enough money for anything "extra" no matter how hard or how much my husband and I worked. That created a huge strain. Money was the thing I could never seem to create. That sense of lack took a lot of the joy and certainly any spontaneity out of life because it was worrisome to have debt hanging over our heads for so long. What is the big thing *you* have been going without, the something that has been blocked?

It wasn't until the seven Abundance Circle tools came to me and I really applied them, along with the secret sauce of standing in a place of observation, not judgment, that the positive shifts finally happened, and in a huge way. Sharing them with the participants in the Abundance Circles I hold in my private psychotherapy practice yields the same results for them. It wasn't necessarily "things" like more money, a new job, or a romantic partner that clients wanted, although those came in for them too. Use of the tools also provided many of them with more peace, self-awareness, or connection with a partner. Many used the word "awakened" to describe the shift the seven tools brought to their lives. They felt more connected to their true selves, more connected to all things, and more present in life. Many described it as feeling they had expanded, and they realized they were playing smaller versions of themselves before learning of these seven tools.

Sometimes they would say they were afraid of "going back" to the way they were before, or worried that the change "wouldn't last." You do not go back to where you started when you have done your inner work, just as you can't unsee something you've seen. It's as if I said to you, "Remember those really, really cute shoes you used to wear in sixth grade? Those were so adorable! Why don't you wear them anymore?" You would look at me bewildered and explain that they no longer fit. Certain ways of being have their time and place in our lives. But sometimes we outgrow them, and they are simply no longer needed.

Playing a smaller version of yourself or living without having and doing the things you are here to have and do, simply no longer fits.

I am so excited for you. Imagine *you*, but untethered by doubt, worry, or limiting stories!

Ready.

Set.

Grow!

BEGINNING EXERCISES

1. Get very clear on what you want to call in with the tools in this book. Is it to create more money and greater financial freedom? A partner? Get very specific about what that looks like to you, down to minute details. Journal about it; how you define your point of desire and what it looks like. Describe how you will know it has arrived and how it feels to you when it does.

2. Do you know what your wounds are? What triggers you? What pushes your buttons? Do you have a sense of why you get triggered by these things in particular and what their origins may be? Pay attention when your buttons are pushed in an "observe, not judge" way and journal about it daily.

CHAPTER 2
TOOL 1: DEEP DESIRE + WORK IN THEORY

You'll see it when you believe it.

—Wayne Dyer

I ONCE HEARD A PERSON say, "I hate lima beans. And I'm glad I hate lima beans. Because if I liked 'em I'd eat 'em and I hate 'em."

Sometimes knowing what you don't want is as important as knowing what you do.

The first tool in manifesting and creating the life of your dreams is getting crystal clear on what it is you want. What is your burning desire, the thing you can't *not* have?

There are two common threads among people who attract what they deeply desire. One is a very clear and deep focus on a goal and the imagining of that goal. The other is relentless tenacity in working to bring that goal into being. This makes perfect sense, doesn't it? When we want something, we get very clear on what it is we want, and then work to make it a reality. This is really a road map for manifesting any of our desires and can be applied to any aspect of life. It works equally well wherever applied.

Most of us have that something we would feel incomplete without. "The thing" that feels etched with desire in our soul. It might be a committed partnership, a baby, a successful career, travel, peace, or a home in the woods. It's different for everyone but we all have something—*the thing*—we daydream and obsess about. That's the "desire" piece. The "work" piece is doing what it takes to make it happen, as in Edison's thousand attempts to create the lightbulb before he succeeded.

When joining one of my Abundance Circles, new participants usually have their own "thing" that has been elusive for years and makes them feel as if their lives are incomplete. Many times, they join not truly believing it can be brought in because they have either gone so long without it and don't want to get their hopes up, or have exhausted many ways to create it and haven't been able to make it happen.

On the other hand, some people feel an immediate "Yes!" to the invitation to join or hear of the circles from past participants and know immediately it is for them too. They feel in their bones that it will be an incredible opportunity—for growth, for calling in their desired object, and for making new friends who will be on the same sort of path. Or they know the Abundance Circles work because they've seen the nearly miraculous shifts in a friend's life.

It's the people who don't quite know what the Circles are, or those who don't quite have the funds to add an eight-session round of group therapy to their budget at the time but do it anyway that I completely marvel at. Because it means letting go of what they do know, even if it isn't working for them ("Maybe if I just work *harder* pushing this stone up a hill, I will get to the top!"), and hoping that what they commit to can work. I see a visual of this as someone on a trapeze who has let go of one bar and hasn't yet grabbed the empty one swinging towards them. Signing up to join an Abundance Circle may feel a bit like that to some. And what if there isn't even a safety net below them? For these people, I suppose "the net" is faith in themselves or in the dream of their desired "thing" versus the abject pain of not having it in their lives.

Here are a few short examples of Abundance Circle participants, and the kinds of stories that have become commonplace for them:

- A working single mom whose ex had taken her to court to stop having to make his child support and alimony payments and who had just been laid off from her job around the same time. Her son, a high school senior, would need a car and money for college tuition very soon. She was feeling panicky about how the money would come in for the things she needed to take care of—all the things that were her responsibility. She was understandably extremely reluctant to start Abundance Circles because of the cost but took the dive and signed up anyway. She is highly intuitive and got a strong inner "Yes" and so, although it was a scary leap and intellectually made "no sense," she signed up. By session number four, she'd been offered a dream job doing work she loved doing and that touched the lives of many people, plus paid her a much, much higher salary than she'd ever made before.

- A woman who wanted to go to Hawaii to visit her grandchildren. She'd been very close to them before they moved there but she had no money to fund the trip. About a month after her Abundance Circle ended, she was suddenly offered an opportunity to move to the very city where her grandchildren lived without even applying for the position. Now she sees her five grandbabies nearly every day! And in paradise on top of it!

- A young private yoga instructor in L.A. who desperately wanted to live in different countries to learn about other cultures but whose monthly budget would be absolutely devastated if she so much as got a parking ticket. She was barely able to pay for groceries and rent and yet she longed to travel and teach. Shortly after she completed her round of the Abundance Circles, she found a long-term paying position teaching yoga in Costa Rica that provided her room and board.

- The Mexican-born actress living in L.A. who deeply desired to win an Emmy for a Spanish-language program—something they hadn't been giving Emmys for when she put one on her vision board—and won one!

Keep reading. Their stories are coming!

These are true accounts, and there are many more: People who not only started the dream projects they had put off for years but completed them before the eight sessions were over, many times by the fourth session. People who found better jobs, better places to live, or long-term romantic relationships that they are still in as of this writing.

Why the big shifts? The tools themselves are powerful. Individually, these tools each merit their own books. In fact, some of them are. Combined, they are even more potent.

What matters is not just that individuals' lives are shifting because what they were seeking is now present in their lives—making them happier, more vital, more fulfilled people—but that their relationships are better too. Larger than that, in terms of the ripple effect it makes for a better world when each of us is doing what is in our heart to do, and when we are aligned, happy, centered, and feeling full and abundant. It's like the difference between trying to do something when our bellies are growling, and we feel depleted and hungry versus when we are satisfied. Obviously, it's much harder to work if we are distracted by lack or if we are running on fumes. So too do we function better in life with our metaphoric bellies full. When we are satisfied with what we have, we are content and joyous.

So, then, what is your "thing?" What would you feel incomplete without, if you never had it in your life? What is "the thing"— the one true thing your heart has been longing to receive in your life for so long—possibly years? Whether it's a long-term, loving, committed relationship, financial abundance, or traveling with your loved one, what does the thought of having that feel like? What emotions well up at the thought of you having or doing it? What has it felt like to go without it all this time?

The biggest lesson I've learned in my own journey, and speaking with people on the same journey, is that getting clear on what you want always includes an "I can't take it anymore!" moment like the one I had regarding shifting my limited abundance beliefs and the idea that I did not have enough for perceived "extras" like travel. *This is a universal turning point.* Everyone has a similar kind of point of no return, where everything begins to shift. It brings the desired goal into laser-sharp focus and the energy for it becomes singular and powerful.

Perhaps you have had such a moment or are close to one. An "I can't take living below my means or skill set" meltdown. An "I can't take not having enough money to do the things I long to do, like visit my grandchildren" moment. Or an "I can't take not sharing my gift with the world in a big way" moment! And there is a big distinction between following up that universal turning point with

"And I guess I'll never have it" versus "And I am getting very close to having it."

I changed my own money story from "There isn't enough and that just is the way it is" to knowing money is just an energy and there is always plenty. My husband's story shifted too. He moved from a place of "not-enoughness" and feeling overwhelmed to being calmer and less stressed around the topic. I know this shift for him wasn't just about more income coming in from me, because when you have a story of lack (money or otherwise), no matter how much you have, it won't feel like enough. Or you might have plenty but worry it won't last. Tim isn't calmer because there is more. There is more because we changed our dance with abundance.

Fear, doubt, and worry no longer sent the message to the Universe that "there isn't enough." Our new message is that there is plenty for all of our needs and always will be, and for that we are deeply grateful. Grateful for the abundance that allows us to handle our expenses with grace and ease and to give freely in ways that feel good to us.

In my experience observing clients for over twenty-five years, the three biggest categories where our "stuff"—or issues—shows up most visibly are money, sex/relationships, and health. This makes sense because they are so important in our lives. When something shows up in one of these categories, it grabs our attention.

What a beautifully designed system, really.

If we aren't receiving the messages we need, or if our abundance-blocking wounds are too hidden for us to know what they are, what better way to get us to pay attention to that inner voice than to stop us in our tracks in a category that really makes us notice.

It's as if our wounded inner child at first whispers a faint "Heyyyy…"–but we didn't hear him or her—and then pokes us with a finger and says it again a little louder: "Hey!" We still might not hear it if we have been conditioned to ignore our feelings. So then our inner child yells, "Hey! Hey! HEY YOU!!!" The voice inside—and the clues on the outside—has to get louder until we stop and give it the attention it deserves.

I have yet to meet someone who says, "Things are going swimmingly in my life. I think it's a good time to go into the deep, dark, hurtful places I have been avoiding all my life."

To want something so badly—for example, to want to be in a deeply committed partnership but be unable to find "The One"—is heartbreaking. To work hard at a job but have bills piling up or land in financial stress feels sickening, even as you do the inner and outer work to be prosperous. To eat well and live a healthy lifestyle yet be chronically unwell or hit with a devastating illness is depressing. Yet this is what happens to so many people. Why? Why is it that for so many people, including maybe you, life can be pretty darn great except for that one big missing thing?

"If only," you say to yourself. "If I just had a partner to share this abundance with!" Or conversely, "If my honey and I just had more money!" And so it goes. This is not a matter of being ungrateful for what you have. These are very real losses in your heart and the longing is true for you. It's as if a dream was placed in your heart when you were born, you've spent your life so far looking for it, and it still isn't there. It feels like a *hole in your soul*.

We all know people like this—or it IS us—the man or woman who is kind, compassionate, funny, intelligent, good-looking, successful, and financially independent, lets his or her friends know to let their friends know they are available, has their profile on online dating sites, and is extremely open when meeting people and yet isn't dating, let alone in a committed relationship, which is their biggest desire in life. Or that man or woman who works hard and long and has for years, and is a dedicated, productive, and steady worker, yet their salary just barely covers living expenses. It's extremely painful. When you have a deep desire within your soul and can't find a way to fulfill it, it is soul-crushing.

So what if you ARE putting both positive thought and energy into something and it still is not coming? What if you are doing everything "right"? You're doing all the outer work. If it's a financial dream, you are working hard to earn money. If it's a relationship you seek, you are letting everyone you know you are looking, you are open to being set up on blind dates, and you are meeting people and going online. What if you're also doing the inner work—you read all the manifesting books, you've created a vision board with pictures of what you want, you've watched *The Secret* ninety-nine times, and still "the thing" hasn't shown up? What do you do then?

You'll have your own "I can't take it anymore!" moment. You'll get mad about it. This is when "the shift hits the fan"! Your "I can't live without this!" It's like an existential crisis but juicier. Because instead of feeling despondent, you feel laser-focused. You will stop at nothing. You can't *not* have it. This will shift *everything*, because you have said it and felt it with such focused clarity and assuredness that the desire in you is now fully revealed and you are willing to do the work in a deeper way than you ever have before.

Sometimes we *think* we are very clear, but we're so focused on getting it "right"—speaking in the present, saying it as if it was already here, saying it as a positive, not a negative, and so on—that our articulated desire may have a softness to it. Or an "if you don't mind" quality. An "if you don't mind"-ness to it.

After your "I can't take it anymore!" moment, there is no question the Universe heard you.

Things on the outside change when things on the inside change.

When I no longer felt victimized by my financial picture but instead was empowered to make it different, the Universe conspired to make it happen and I received support to make it happen.

This will happen with your own big yes to receiving what your heart has longed for.

CHAPTER 3
TOOL 1: DEEP DESIRE + WORK
IN PRACTICE

ENERGY MUST BE APPLIED IN a physical, or worldly, way. When we hit a block in reaching our goal, thereby not attracting the very thing we want most, it isn't because we don't know the next step. It isn't that we don't know what to do. We know exactly what we need to do! We know the next step very well and it scares us. The "work" piece in this chapter is facing your fear and doing it anyway.

Thinking about your desired outcome is not enough to make things happen, although it's the first component. The last six letters of *attraction* are *action*. You must have *action* behind the thought as well. Thinking without action is just dreaming.

That might show up as reading books on the subject of the "thing" you are trying to pull in, such as *Think and Grow Rich* or *You Are a Badass at Money* and similar books if what you desire is more financial abundance. Or it could be trying online dating or going on blind dates and letting friends know you are looking—even when that feels intimidating, embarrassing, or vulnerable—if what you want is to meet a romantic partner. Or it could be considering adoption or arduous fertility treatment if what you desire is a baby and it has not happened after an extended period of trying.

It could also be noticing that, if the thing you want is marriage, but you have a habit of saying or thinking "I don't trust women/men," then your job is to tend to your inner work by changing that belief so you are no longer sending the Universe a mixed message. Your deeply held beliefs and your habits must match what it is you say you want to attract. This is the Law of Action.

The "work" stage is any *action* you take in the direction of your desire. And it doesn't have to feel like work, although it may pull you out of your comfort zone to do it! It can be play, like making a beautiful vision board, or journaling, or writing your desire on Post-it notes and posting them throughout your home. The "work" stage is the piece that brings your deep inner desire and personal growth to the outside.

The dominant thoughts we hold in our mind act like a magnet as we pull our desires into our lives, so it's important to get very clear. Define your desire in a way that excites you and that you believe can happen. And remember that the Universe does not care about the size or amount, so go for it!

Here is how we access that in the very first session of the Abundance Circles. I ask the participants to close their eyes and have them start imagining their desired object or outcome (or as I say, "The Thing" they want to attract). I remind them that it is important that they not only see it in their mind, but also *feel* it. I ask, "What would it feel like to have your desire in your life? What might that look like? What does it smell like? Can you touch it? Who is there cheering you on when you have it?"

I have at least a vague sense of what they want to manifest from what they wrote on the Abundance Circle application before starting their round of circles. I use some of what I know to help create a "picture."

"If it's an Oscar you want—or any award for that matter—who is in the audience watching you receive it? Look at their smiling faces as you hold the statue for the first time! Is it heavier than you had imagined? If it's a cabin in the woods, what does the space look and feel like? Can you smell the pine trees or logs burning in the fireplace? If it's giving talks on a subject you are passionate about, who is in the audience? Imagine seeing them mesmerized by your words, nodding in agreement, and giving you a standing ovation."

I give them moments of pause between these questions and allow them time to really get clear. Then I slowly close the meditation and ask them to open their eyes.

There is a moment to collect themselves and "come back" to the room from wherever their imaginations took them, and then I ask them to write in their journals what they saw and experienced in their imaginations. Writing things down after hearing or seeing something not only gives us a place to return to and be reminded of things we might otherwise miss or forget (that's why taking notes in a class is a good idea!), but it's been proven that writing, which uses a different part of the brain than thinking, helps us retain much better *because* we access two distinct parts of the brain when we both visualize or hear something, and then write it.

Next, I ask them to share what they saw. Speaking about our dream helps anchor it deeper still. Speaking it to others gives it more weight than it would have if we kept it to ourselves, and makes us feel somehow more accountable to keep striving to call it in. In addition, the enthusiastic reaction of the others to each person sharing helps to concretize the shared dreams, like invisible scaffolding holding up each vision. The participants can absolutely see these visions for each other, and very often also have ideas for making them happen that those sharing might not have thought of before.

To harness the positivity from the Abundance Circle's first gathering and to really keep it going after the session, I have the participants review their description of what came up in the meditation and other notes from the session when they get home. At home, your desired manifestation can be reinforced with visual cues, such as pictures of what you want to manifest in your workspace. As one example, if it's a romantic partner you seek, place images of romantic-looking couples on a vision board where you will see them every day.

These steps are the foundation for calling in your deeply desired dream.

It's important that you not only see your defined desire in your mind, but also feel it.

What makes most people fail to bring in what they say they want is their lack of understanding of the Law of Resonance. This means, when you have a desire and think about it, it creates a certain vibration or "resonance" in you. Just thinking of it elevates your vibration. Imagine the feeling when you are in love. Or when you imagine a trip to Italy! Or moving into a new house that is exactly what you need.

But we do not tend to stay focused on that and the energy around it dissipates, causing the vibration to lower. Life happens. We get distracted by the laundry that needs to be washed. The bills that need to be paid. The dog that needs to be walked. Our thoughts and our priorities wander to other things. When we are no longer consciously focused on our desire, our deeply held, unconscious, possibly negative and possibly counterproductive beliefs are now running the show. What we really want working are the trillions of cells in our body holding the vision and vibrating on it positively on an unconscious level. That is why the inner work piece is so important: it will make conscious any sabotaging, unconscious inner dialogue that thwarts what we say we want.

The conscious mind makes the choices, but the unconscious mind implements those choices. Therefore, you must have your conscious and unconscious aligned in a coherent pattern. They must square up.

The Law of Resonance (or "vibration") is the law that assures that all energy continuously vibrates at a given frequency and attracts conditions, circumstances, and people into our lives.

What determines this resonance that you emit from your physical body is your emotions.

One of the most powerful and effective ways for taking conscious control over your thoughts and emotions is through meditation. Meditation has been scientifically proven to change the resonance of the human physiology. It creates a sense of peace, calm, and well-being. As a result, this sense of calm automatically changes the resonance or vibrational frequency that an individual projects into the world, thereby attracting more pleasurable and more desirable things and situations into their lives.

Meditation also balances the left and right hemispheres of the brain, creating "whole brain thinking," which dramatically reduces unfocused "monkey mind" brain activity. This creates more and higher awareness and enhances intuition. It gives us a deeper understanding and appreciation of our connection to each other and for life and the unseen.

If this sounds too "woo-woo," think about this: Aren't there people you like to hang out with and other people, not so much? Are there people you gravitate toward and those you don't? What is the difference? Plain and simple, it's their energy. People with good energy feel good to be around! They are warm, nonjudgmental, kind, open. We are always emitting vibrations of our own and "reading" other people and situations as well. Becoming aware of this Law of Resonance is key to bringing in what you deeply desire. This is what the Mexican-born actress living in L.A., who wanted to win an Emmy for a Spanish language program, did! She kept the positivity dial around her object of desire set to extra high. More about how she did it is coming.

One Abundance Circle participant wanted to manifest marriage. She was very clear about the kind of guy she wanted to be with. He would share her love of the ocean and the outdoors, like her children, and be funny, loyal, social, and athletic. One day, she finished surfing and when she came out of the water, a guy who had been watching her surf approached her and said hello. She greeted him back and asked him how he was. He said, "Good, *now!*" That was seven years ago, and they have been together ever since! It was "the guy" from her vision. He loves the ocean, loves her children, and is funny, loyal, and social. But she jokes that she forgot to add "Democrat" to her wish list and says, half-jokingly, "He's a *Republican!*"

When I mention this story in groups, participants laugh, but then sometimes get a little panicked, like they have to think of everything. The truth is, you don't. If it was important to our surfer that her dream guy was a Democrat, she would have put that on her list. In her case, their difference of opinion in politics is not a deal-breaker. If it was, she wouldn't have left it off.

A member of one Abundance Circle always said that "getting married" was the thing she wanted to pull in to make her life feel more complete. She was successful, had her own home by the time she was in her late twenties, and was funny, beautiful, passionate, and kind. She let her friends know she was looking and that she was open to being set up on dates. She was also on several dating sites. But she wasn't meeting men or dating, let alone planning to get married, and she wanted a partner to share her life with.

One day, in one of my Abundance Circles, I noticed that when she stated again that she wanted to get married, she made a face. It was subtle. Very subtle. I asked her about it, and it turned out she'd been married once before, very briefly and without children, and it was not a good experience for her. She spoke of how controlled she felt by her former husband and that she'd lost her freedom and her voice.

I said, "Then maybe you don't really want to get married. Could that be true? That you think, 'If it looks like *that,* I want nothing to do with it'?" Her eyes misted up and she said quietly, "Yes. I believe that's true."

So I said, "Well, it seems to me there are two things you can do now that you have that awareness. In calling it into your life, you can change the word 'marriage' to being together in a lifelong live-in, committed (but not married) relationship and continue to ask for that to come into your life the way you used to say you wanted 'marriage.' Or you can use the word 'marriage,' but change your vision of marriage to one that doesn't look and feel like the last one: one in which you share your life with a partner you deeply love, still have your freedom and your voice, and are blissfully happy."

Upon receiving that clarity, she broadened her definition and her vision of having a man in her life. Within a short time, she had met and was dating three eligible men she liked a lot. Now it was "raining men" for her! Alleluia!

When she became conscious of her negative feelings about marriage, she was able to dissociate her feelings about her last marriage from her ideas about all marriages. She reframed marriage as a long-term, loving relationship with a caring partner, thereby removing the unconscious block she had about marriage being about giving up one's autonomy. With more clarity on what marriage would be like and the kind of man she could have that with, she got clear on the "order" she wanted to place to the Universe. That created a huge shift in her life.

This is what you must always do when placing your order to the Universe. It's vital to be clear about what you want—and what you do not want as well—and to check for any place inside of you that might not really desire that. If you have unconscious objections, it will be like driving with one foot on the gas and one on the brake. After the once-unhappily married participant got clear that marriage could be all she imagined, her energy around it shifted. That's when the line formed at her front door!

I once met a beautiful, happily married couple at a party. They had an amazing chemistry. I asked how they met. The wife told me that years prior, she had dated quite a bit and became burned out after so many years without finding a wonderful, committed man. She no longer wished to keep going on lots of dates with different men and was ready to "settle down," so she decided to take a year off to "date herself." She would just get to know herself better, grow, study, and become the best version of herself without dating for one year. She wanted to meet The One eventually and felt he was getting ready for her out there somewhere as well.

So she did her own self-development and inner growth work and said no to any man who asked her out in that period. But in the meantime, she hung up a man's robe, size medium, in her closet and put a pair of men's slippers, size 11, by her bed. She bought some nicely scented men's cologne and sprayed it in her room at night. The whole time she was working on becoming a better her, she also called in her beloved, silently putting out the message that she was getting herself ready for him. Not long after the year was up, she met a man. The man I met at the party. They dated, fell in love, and married. And now he wears the slippers and robe, both of which fit him perfectly. Oh, and he also wears and loves the cologne!

Another woman in one of my Abundance Circles had been in a marriage for six years, but her husband had an affair and the marriage ended. She was devastated by his infidelity and took the time she needed to heal her hurt, pain, and confusion. When she was ready to meet another man, she wrote a list of qualities (a "Requirement

List") she sought in the man she wanted to call in. Obviously, she wanted him to be trustworthy, committed, and faithful. And kind. He had to do the things she loves to do, enjoy travel, and be conscious, sensitive, and have similar political and social values. He had to love her cats and be a vegetarian.

She listed very specific qualities because she didn't want to get into a relationship and suffer disappointment again. She was ready for mature, deep, committed, and lasting love, so she was quite clear what her deep desire was. As for the "work" aspect, she tried online dating, although that was extremely uncomfortable for her, and she did go on some dates. She allowed friends to set up blind dates as well. Both were far outside her comfort zone, but she did them anyway.

Sometimes she would bring photos to the Abundance Circle of the men she was introduced to or met online and tell us a little about them and how the dates were coming along. One evening, she brought in the profile photo of a guy named Theo.

As soon as I saw his picture, I remember a very clear voice in my head saying "That's *The One*. That's The One she is going to be with." I didn't say that out loud because I didn't want to freak her out, but the voice could not have been clearer. I said instead, "Ohh. I *like* him! I think you should give it a try!"

It took some prompting from the group for her to go out with him and give it a try because, although she felt drawn to him from his profile and the little bit of conversation they'd had up to that point, she had met him online. That one piece made her uneasy and caused her to question her intuition about him. But she did go out with him. Now, six years after she brought his photo in to show us, they are still together. He shares her world views and is loyal, vegetarian, handsome, and kind. They have been to seven countries together and counting. They bought a house together. And he loves her cats.

* * *

THE DEEP DESIRE PORTION OF manifesting is a bit tricky in that it requires a certain finesse or hitting a "sweet spot." This means connecting with your feelings and getting into the mindset of your deep desire. Picturing it in detail. Imagining having it. "Trying on" what it would feel like to have it in your life, bringing your emotions into it, and so on. You must once again make conscious choices about your thoughts and energy. Your thoughts around it must be a steadfast desire and belief you will have it, but should not include begging, *no matter how badly you want it.* That is what I mean when I say you need to hit the "sweet spot."

If you think and say something like, "Please, please, please, please, Universe! I *neeeeeed* this!"—what you will create is *needing.* Not the completion of *having.* A pleading energy can actually repel your deep desire, whereas a quiet confidence that it is on its way can bring it in.

You must deeply desire it and believe that it is on its way. Do your inner and outer work to that end. Then you must ask for it in a way that doesn't actually propel it further from you but invites it in, knowing it's yours. You want to come at it from this perspective: "I am receiving good health/a partner/financial freedom"—whatever it is you deeply desire to pull in— *"with grace and ease."* Or picture what you desire, feel it as if it is happening right now, and say, "I am so richly enjoying my health/my beloved/my abundance." Say it in the present tense and say it as if it's just the truth, casually and without a lot of attachment, while also letting yourself feel the joy of having it.

As photographer Jill Paider, author of twenty books on fine photography, world traveler, and Abundance Circle member, said, "Manifesting is essentially a yin-yang balance between taking action and letting the Universe do its work. You can't will it entirely, nor can you sit on the couch and wait for it to happen."

It's like that old joke about the man in the horrible flood. He refused all the help sent his way, saying "God will save me." The floodwaters rose higher and higher and he climbed up to his rooftop, where a helicopter spotted him and dropped a rope ladder. A rescue officer came down the ladder and pleaded with the man, "Grab my hand and I will pull you up!" But the man still refused. "No thanks. God will save me!" Of course, he died in the flood and when he got to heaven, he saw God and said, "I don't understand. I had faith in you to come save me. Why didn't you come?"

And God said, "I sent you a car, a canoe, a motorboat, and a helicopter. What more did you want?"

You must receive the help the Universe sends you and do some work yourself.

An example of desiring something, stating it, and then letting it go happened to me in a big way before I knew of the power of this tool. It happened very organically and with little effort, which is why it happened. This is an example of the "sweet spot" I described.

One afternoon, my husband and I went to the gym and on our way out saw a cute car in the gym parking lot that I had never seen before. It was a silver 2002 Audi TT. They were new then, and we both thought it was adorable, if you can say that about a car. We walked around and admired it, and although I had a car I liked and wasn't in the market for a new one, I said, "I love that car! I would love to have that!"

Very shortly after that, one of my husband's clients was moving to Paris and had to sell his possessions quickly. He offered to sell his car at a very discounted price. He hadn't heard we were looking and in fact, we really weren't. But the man asked us anyway. It was a silver 2002 Audi TT, the same year, color, and model as the one we had admired in the gym parking lot. We bought it and I love it. I named my German car "Otto" (pronounced of course, "Auto!").

The Deep Desire + Work phase is equal parts deeply wanting and focusing on something: love, a relationship, financial abundance, a promotion, peace, travel, whatever it is to you—plus the inner and outer work you need to do—and then letting it go as you trust it is on its way.

Get clear on your picture of it, and then add, "*This or something better.*" Take an "I receive this or something better" stance. This way, you aren't limiting what the Universe sends your way!

So to write your own deep desire, here are some templates to help you get started:

1. I am ready to receive a two-bedroom, light-filled home with a large backyard and a lot of trees that is within my budget, twelve miles or less from work. (You could add specifics about the home here: the exact price point, the style of home, the type of neighborhood or street it is on, the size of its rooms. The direction it faces. The presence of wonderful neighbors. Quiet. And things like "hardwood floors" or "has a lot of privacy.")

2. I am open to meeting a single man ready for a romantic relationship who is funny, honest, kind, loyal, creative, and shares my love for being outdoors. (You could add specifics about this person here, like what he looks like, does for a living and for hobbies, books he likes, and so on. Get creative!)

3. I am receiving three new enthusiastic, kick-ass clients who are open to possibilities and willing to listen to my suggestions, work diligently, and pay my full fee willingly. (Again, you can get more specific here to really nail it.)

Here, in her words, is the exquisitely beautiful example of this happening with a participant in one of my Abundance Circles, Mexican-born actor, writer, and producer Iran Daniel, whose story of a dream come true I teased you with before:

I do a dream board every year in January. In 2009, I included an Emmy and a star on a red carpet and I realized that's what I wanted. To be an Emmy winner. Later that year, I took on a job as entertainment reporter for a national Hispanic network doing celebrity interviews. One of my assignments was to cover the Emmy Awards and I remember standing on that red carpet, thinking, "One day I will be an Emmy winner." And nothing was going to cloud my vision of that accomplishment. I know if I had shared that with anyone, it would have sounded silly because here I was, just a little Hispanic entertainment reporter, interviewing A-listers on the red carpet and dreaming of having an Emmy. I mean, it's silly! Especially since the Academy of Television Arts and Sciences *only* awards English speaking shows!

Two years later, some upper management from the TV network came from Miami to L.A. to have a meeting with all the West Coast staff and letting us know of a few changes in the way they wanted us to do things. Before the meeting ended, they told us they didn't want to just come and tell us what to do. They wanted us to share with them our deepest dreams and they were going to try to help us achieve them. In all honesty, the sentiment was cute, but this company wasn't one to help their employees out at all. Still, we all shared.

Some shared that they wanted to be the hosts of their own TV show; others wanted to produce. The executive kept writing down all the employees' dreams as if to prepare a letter to Santa by the end of the year.

When my turn came, I told the executive I wanted to win an Emmy. The entire room stared at me like I had just said I wanted to be the CEO of the network. Anyway, the executive wrote down my dream but took a long pause and said, "Hmm...an Emmy...let me see when the submission deadline is."

That was the last time I talked about it. I left the network for health reasons at the end of 2013.

In early 2014, I got a mention on a Twitter post by a colleague from the network saying that for the first time in history, the Academy of Television Arts and Sciences was including Spanish-speaking morning TV shows and we were nominated for the category.

Mid-November 2014, we won.

I had my dream. I had my Emmy!

One day cleaning my apartment in early 2015, I found my 2010 dream board in a closet and I almost fainted when I saw the little Emmy statuette I had included in my dreams. You never know when they might just come true. Even if they seem impossible when you first desire them.

* * *

WHEN YOU ARE CLEAR ON what it is your heart and your soul deeply desire, when you can imagine and *feel* it in your life, when you've done your inner and outer work to create it happening, and when you have released it to the Universe in a "This or something better," or an "I trust it's on its way" kind of energy, you will be ready for Tool 2 and to say, "Beep! Beep! Get out of my way!"

But before you go on to the next tool, do the work part of this tool to get the proverbial ball rolling! The Universe is waiting for instructions from you. When you place your "order" with a little work and energy behind it, you create a stronger message.

So, let's go!

* * *

Many people fail in life, not for lack of ability or brains or even courage, but simply because they have never organized their energies around a goal.

—Elbert Hubbard

DEEP DESIRE + WORK EXERCISE: VISUALIZING WHAT YOU WANT TO ATTRACT

First, sit comfortably in a quiet place with your feet flat on the floor and your arms gently resting by your sides. Take a few deep breaths, releasing tension as you exhale.

Begin to imagine "The Thing" you want to bring in. Perhaps you picture different scenarios and choose the best elements from each one. Get crystal clear on the fine details. Also, envision that it comes to you easily, "with grace and ease." Use that phrase. Imagine doors opening easily for you to receive what you desire. Although the Universe doesn't set limits on the size, amount, or time frame of what we want to pull in—we do that by ourselves—it should be something you believe can happen. If you ask for it but don't see it as possible, you send a conflicting message. Get clear on a message that is believable to you.

If your dream is speaking onstage and spreading your powerful message to the world, for example, envision yourself onstage looking and feeling great. What are you wearing? Who is in the audience? Imagine people in the audience looking moved by and interested in the things you say. Now scan the audience more closely and see a beloved supporter beaming up at you. It could be someone whose presence makes you feel comfortable and happy, whether they are alive or have already passed, or someone you simply admire in the world. Maybe they have their hand on their heart in a loving gesture that says they are moved by you, or proud of you. What's on the stage with you? Is there a screen behind you? If so, is there anything on it? Is there bottle of San Pellegrino sparkling water on the podium? A panel of other experts sitting behind you? Are you speaking in a theater with plush red velvet seats and architectural details? Or is it a cool, modern room with floor-to-ceiling glass windows in a contemporary building? Or are you sitting across from Oprah, being interviewed? How large is the audience? Is there a smell associated with the place? Any background music? Or is it completely quiet, with all eyes and ears on you? What are some of the key points you make? How are you feeling up there? Really feel it now. Get into the feeling you hope to have and experience it right now. Bringing your awareness to the emotional component you will experience when it is happening is key. *It's vital you allow yourself to feel in your imagination how it will feel when it occurs.* Make it a vibrational match.

If it's a car you want, think about how it feels to drive it. Does it have a new car smell? What does the seat beneath you feel like? How fast or carefully are you driving the car? What color is it? What year, make, and model? What does it look like from the outside? From the inside? Where do you take it? What does the door handle feel like in your hand when you open it to slip into the front seat and drive?

If it is financial freedom and abundance you seek, what is the amount you want? Literally, the amount. What does that amount translate to in weekly, monthly, yearly amounts? What do you intend to do with it? What is some of the good you will do with it? What causes or charities could you give to and how does it *feel* when you think of giving to them? When you come up with a figure that feels right, how does having that amount make you feel? How much money do you want to carry around in your wallet at all times, *minimally?* Visualize it. See yourself opening up your wallet to pay for something beautiful and finely made at an expensive store you love. See yourself pulling out cash to pay for it, with plenty left in the wallet. Carry around more than you are used to having in "real time." Every time you see it, you are reminded of your wealth.

Unsure of the amount you think you want? What would give you enough to pay off your bills, live the life you want, give to charities you believe in, and have enough for retirement? That number is a good place to start.

If you don't desire money per se, but something money will buy you, your particular Deep Desire work might be to figure out a way to make that come to life instead of attracting the money for it.

* * *

You are never given a wish without also being given the power to make it come true. You may have to work for it, however.

—Richard Bach, *Illusions: The Adventures of a Reluctant Messiah*

THE WORK COMPONENT: MAKING IT HAPPEN

WHEN YOU HAVE GOTTEN CLEAR on what it is you want, you are ready for the work stage of Deep Desire + Work. I cannot underscore enough the importance of your knowing what you really want and defining it for yourself in very specific language. If you are not clear, the Universe can't be either. Your metaphoric radio signal will be fuzzy and you will feel frustrated. *This is where most people get stuck and frustrated when trying to manifest what they want in life.* Your goal needs to be believable to you, and you need to allow yourself enough time to achieve it. Enough time, but not too much time—that can sabotage your focus on reaching your goal. If you don't get this part of the seven tools down, the rest won't work for you. This is your foundation.

Outer work includes learning everything you can on the topic of the thing you want to call in, and possibly meeting with people already doing it if that's applicable. It includes going out of your comfort zone and being courageous on your quest, even when your knees are knocking. And it includes "play" like making vision boards.

The following exercises on the work piece of Deep Desire + Work give you concrete things to do that will help magnetize your desire or goal to you. It's called work but think of it as play. Enjoy these exercises! Get juiced! You'll feel geared up to put your desires into action and feel excited, and *that* is attractive! Being attractive will draw more positivity to you. Yum! Who doesn't want *that*? Are you feeling excited?!

DEEP DESIRE: DO YOUR INNER WORK

I'VE MENTIONED "DOING YOUR INNER work" throughout this book. This is one of the most important tasks in bringing in what you want. You only attract what you're ready to receive. Being your best means you attract the best. Just ask the woman who only dated herself for a year, worked on herself, and attracted her beloved soul mate.

But what does doing your inner work mean exactly? It means looking at your limiting beliefs, healing your wounds, removing blocks, and rewriting faulty stories. Many of them aren't true, you know, even if they feel like they are.

In order to receive all we deserve and desire, live full authentic lives, and form healthy relationships, we need to heal the limiting and often unconscious beliefs about ourselves we took on from our childhood. Without understanding this, we are doomed to repeat our dysfunctional patterns or continue playing small. Healing our hurts or removing the blocks that prevent us from showing up most fully through therapy or other modalities of healing creates a life that feels freer and more authentic.

Observe, don't judge: How clear are you able to get on what it is you desire to attract into your life, and on the amount of work and focus you will put toward that goal?

DO YOUR OUTER WORK

Do AT LEAST FIVE OF the following Outer Work exercises. The rest, consider food for thought; food for your abundance slow cooker!

1. **Create a vision board or life map.**

Seeing (it every day on a board!) is believing. Create a vision board or life map with pictures of your goal or dream, and the way you want to feel, by cutting out photos of your deep desire from magazines. Put the board or map in a place where you will see it every day. Or create a Pinterest board with images of your heart's desire. Seeing it frequently will have you imagining it and believing it possible. Making a vision board can be especially fun when you do it with other friends working on their own boards at the same time. Gather a couple of friends and have a vision board party.

Pick a color or scene that you like for the background and attach words and pictures that inspire you or represent the life you want to create. Words like *love, prosperity, happiness, success,* and *joy* are some examples. Your board should represent the way you want to feel, not just material things, but put those material things up too! If you have photos from vacations, objects from nature, or a charm from a friend, put those on too—if they evoke warm, positive feelings that you want more of.

A study looking at brain patterns in weightlifters found that the patterns activated when a weightlifter lifted hundreds of pounds were similarly activated when they only imagined lifting. This gives new meaning to the expression, "Imagine that!"

When you're finished, put the board in a place where you will see it often and where it will bring you joy. Above your desk might be a good spot.

There are many online links on how to create vision boards and life maps, so choosing one that resonates with your personality or style should be easy. There is no wrong way to do this.

When what you ask for shows up in tangible form and you can see it right now in your life, you will shift from "seeing is believing" to "believing is seeing"!

2. **Write.**

Write down your goals or desires. Feel as if they have already happened. It is the feeling that galvanizes energy. As Albert Einstein said, "Everything is energy and that's all there is to it."

Write your goals and desires in journals and go back and reread your previous entries so you can see how far you have come. It's okay to have goals for several categories: health, wealth, travel, relationship, and so on.

Besides journaling, write on Post-its so that you can see your desires every day. Put them on the dashboard in your car, on your computer, on your fridge, and on your bathroom mirror. And when you see them, feel how excited you are—as if they are present in your life this very moment.

3. **Step out of your comfort zone.**

Another key "Work" component is stepping out of your comfort zone. We are wired for comfort, which is why it's hard to let go of it. Our comfort zone is where we feel most at home. "We pay a heavy price for our fear of failure," wrote John Gardner. "It is a powerful obstacle to growth. It assures the progressive narrowing of the personality and prevents exploration and experimentation. There is no learning without some difficulty and fumbling." I would add that there is little chance for manifesting the life we want without stepping out of our comfort zone as well. We may have to ask our boss for a raise. Or ask a person we are attracted to out on a date. Or explore new, alternative spiritual practices or take classes in something that stretches our thinking if what we want to attract is more expansiveness in life.

4. **Reach out to people.**

Reach out to people who can help you bring your vision into real time.

If you desire a partner, let your family and friends know you are looking and would be willing to be set up. That may be scary. (See Number 3!) If it's a new job, don't be afraid to approach people in the industry or people you know who may have contacts in it.

5. **Investigate and research ways to make your dream a reality.**

If your desire is to travel abroad and get to know other cultures, you could focus on making enough money to make that happen or you could manifest it happening in other ways. Maybe your task is to find internships or jobs in other countries. A quick Google search brings up many links to travel and work or study abroad.

Or if traveling as a tourist is the thing you want to bring in more of, see how to travel on the cheap. Use a credit card that gives you travel miles for flights and hotel points. Get a job on a cruise line. I know five people who have worked for them and traveled all over the world. Sign up on airline mailing lists. They offer 2-for-1 specials, discounts on flights, and more. WWOOFing (World Wide Opportunities on Organic Farms) gives you free room and board while working on farms all over the world. Consider voluntourism. (That's volunteer + tourism.) Sites such as www.Voluntourism.org, www.ProjectsAbroad.org, and www.GlobeAware.org are some examples.

Airbnb is another way to travel cheaply. Airbnb is a great way to find a sweet place to stay on your vacation, and putting your own home on Airbnb can help you fund your travels. You can earn back the money you spent on your accommodations while you are away!

All of this is to say that there are ways to make your desire a reality with a little creativity, and by getting very clear on your deep desire and then doing some work to make it happen. I have noticed through watching my Abundance Circle participants that when they get crystal clear on what they desire, ideas for how to make that happen start formulating in their minds.

Whatever your goal is—a six- or seven-figure income, a relationship, a fit and healthy body, starting a blog, or writing a book—investigate the *how* behind that. Put your energy into it. What we focus on grows. Get bloody excited about your "thing"! Tell everyone you know about what you want. Their positive energy will be added to yours, making it exponentially more powerful. Plus, they may know of something or someone that will help you along your way.

Learn as much as you can about what you want to bring in.

Let's use the example of the car I mentioned earlier. Research everything you can on it. Look at pictures of it online. You could put a picture of it on your screensaver. If you know someone who has the exact make and model of the car you want, ask them about it. Is there a way to test drive the car?

Or if it's public speaking you want to do, consider a two-fold approach to the research side. Imagine the places you want to speak and do some research on them. Research, also, the *how* of speaking. What made Martin Luther King, Jr. such an amazing and successful speaker? What could you learn about public speaking by studying him? What could you emulate?

If it's a trip to Italy, where do you want to go specifically? Study the language and become at least conversationally competent for when you go. Do a little research on the history and culture.

6. Take daily actions that support your goals.

Deep desire without the work piece is just dreaming. You need to take action on a daily basis to bring it in, whether it's getting fit, making more money, finding a partner, deepening your spiritual practice, or whatever.

Answer this question daily: "What is one thing I can be and do today to support my desire?"

When you are in a new, exciting, on-fire relationship with a person you love deeply and desire, do you ignore them? Or do you give them attention every day? Do you think of that person constantly? Maybe let them know that you do? Hmm? I am guessing, yes. So why wouldn't you do that with your goal? Treat your goal as you would your beloved.

CHAPTER 4
TOOL 2: THE FINESSE OF RECEIVING

THE LIVE ABUNDANCE CIRCLES THAT inspired this book are held every other week for eight sessions. In each session, one of each of the seven abundance tools is presented and discussed fully. This gives ample time to discuss each tool during the gatherings, as well as time to assimilate the tool between meetings and put them into practice. Every abundance tool builds on the one before it.

Each of the seven tools in this book is sure to bring up your own stories, blocks, memories, and curiosity. Feel free to take your time between chapters to really dive deep into what the tool means to you, what your relationship to the tool has been up until now, how you might use it in your life going forward, and how you can leverage it to create the kind of life you have dreamt for yourself.

Consider really focusing on one tool per week, even if you understand the tool and feel like doing more or incorporating the other tools. And ask yourself if you spent some time on the Deep Desire + Work tool before beginning this chapter. It's important to practice each one to really get to know it. Become intimate with it and make note of when things shift and you find yourself using it as second nature kind. Making mental notes of using a tool will help you develop and integrate the habit of using it.

For example, in the last chapter, one suggested example of doing the "work" piece was to ask people for help in the field of your goal. If you find you are now able to do that without being nervous or having to think about it first, that's great! Take note of that. Would it always have been easy or are you feeling more emboldened to ask for what you need?

Also, what "inner" work did you apply to that tool? Did you change your thoughts to be positive and in the present when you focus on pulling what you desire into your life? The "inner" piece is what you *feel and think* about regarding your goal. Have you given more full-body awareness to that goal? Really seen, felt, imagined, tasted, and smelled it as if it were here, right now? "Inner" work also means paying attention to any stories or limiting beliefs you hold onto about yourself. I'll get to how to heal those wounds and reverse the limiting stories and beliefs later, but for now, just being aware of them and questioning them is enough.

What "outer" work did you do? Did you do anything outside your comfort zone to try to bring in the thing you desire? If so, you have already experienced a "pattern interrupt"! You did something outside your old paradigm of behavior to get closer to your goal. "Pattern interrupts" are *huge*.

Have you looked deeper into the subject matter of what you want to call in? For example, by signing up for Italian lessons if you want to travel to Italy or acting classes if you want to become an actor, or picking up a book on relationships if you want to call in a better relationship? Have you started an exercise program or begun being mindful of the foods you eat if you want a healthier body? Have you created a vision board or posted your goals where you can see them? These are all examples of doing the "outer" work. It's the visible, tangible things you *do* that are the "outer" work piece. Your buying and reading this book is an example of the outer work piece of Deep Desire + Work.

Imagine that each tool is a piece of chocolate. Imagine a gorgeous plate of the finest chocolates. Maybe they're backlit by sunshine coming in through a window. The chocolates look tempting and you cannot resist. You pick one up. Don't just grab and eat it without savoring it or swallow without enjoying its decadence. Bring it up to your nose and smell it. Close your eyes. Inhale the scent *slowly*. Take the chocolate and glide it haltingly along your lips. Really feel and smell that and "tease" your lips with it. Part your lips and place it gently on your tongue. Let it pause there a moment. Feel it softly melt in your mouth. Feel the almost-divine quality of it warming your mouth in delicious splendor. Taste it fully before swallowing.

Let *that* be how you experience and expand your abundance with these tools. Fully. On their own. In delicious splendor. After you have become clear about what your heart deeply desires, you need to be able to receive it—and all the other good the Universe sends your way. If you have difficulty receiving, you won't be able to let it in when it comes. That may seem obvious, but many of us do not do well with receiving and are more practiced at rejecting than we are at allowing.

Let me be clear: Receiving is not about getting. It's about allowing. Many of us are poor receivers. We reject help on a regular basis. It's even hard to receive a compliment. We feel the need to negate whatever we were complimented on, rejecting the gift someone just handed us. If someone compliments our hair or clothes, or the impact we are having, a job well done or the meal we just made, we somehow feel the need to tell them why it really isn't special.

Dolly Parton once said that, as a girl, she'd see her female relatives spend days preparing a meal and when their guests complimented them on it, they would say, "Oh, this? It's just something I had on hand and whipped up!"

Once I was at a friend's house with some other women and one woman looked especially good in her jeans. When we all said so, she rejected the compliment with an "Oh, my God. You wouldn't say that if you saw me naked. You should see my cellulite."

Now why do we do that?

Why is it somehow easier to put ourselves down and paint a picture of our cellulite in others' minds? Why is it so hard for us to just smile and say thank you? Because we think, erroneously, that saying thank you is the equivalent of saying, "I know. I'm pretty hot stuff," when someone tells us something nice. It isn't (not that there'd be anything wrong with that, actually!). It's simply saying, "I appreciate your kind words." It is receiving their gift graciously.

Consider where you have difficulty receiving in your own life. In general, how are you at receiving help and compliments? Do you decline them or accept them with gratitude?

Receiving is the flip side of giving. We can't have one without the other. It's like breath or the tide.

Breathing and tides both go in and out—not just out. There is balance to the ebb and flow of life, and to the in and out of breath. If we only exhaled, we would die. Sometimes we may think that receiving is showing our weakness or vulnerability, when it's actually just being gracious and grateful.

Sometimes life puts us in a position of *having* to receive.

Joya Petra Gallasch is a lovely friend of mine and an author, coach, and international workshop and retreat leader. Originally from Munich, Germany, she has lived in the U.S. since 1988.

On September 12, 2015, she lost her home, workshop space, beloved cat, and everything she owned—thirty years of her past—in a devastating wildfire in Lake County in northern California. The fire destroyed more than 1,400 homes and structures and seventy-four thousand acres of land, including the entire Boggs National

Forest—more than fifty thousand acres of land. Residents were suddenly rendered homeless. Fortunately, more than seventeen thousand people were safely evacuated with very little warning.

Joya lost all of her writings, her art, her clothes, her furniture, gifts from friends from all over the world, and gifts she had wrapped in advance to give others. *Everything.* The destruction was not only of her own home, but of the whole neighborhood and the beloved forest she lived in. Everything was destroyed.

On top of her loss, she had no homeowner's insurance because she was told by five different insurance companies that her home was too close to the precious old-growth trees to insure.

Through all of this devastation, Joya came away with many gifts. One that stands out is the gift of learning how to receive. This is how she describes it.

All my belongings, art, and workshop inventory were cremated. I could not get insurance. I was told that the majestic, tall, ancient trees, my guardians for five years, were too close to the house. I had to forgive myself for not having called every insurance company in the country. After all the healing work I did on this land, I believed a fire would never happen to me. For many months, I felt ashamed and blamed myself. I got stuck in grief and deep depression. Day by day, I was invited to stay present, to feel fully, to be in the not-knowing—and to trust.

One of my greatest gifts in this "letting go adventure" has been the gift of receiving.

I love presents. I love to find them and give them to others. I had a huge gift box with many presents for friends and family. A present is like a piece of presence, love, and heart of myself that I get to share. My big box of presents to give to loved ones burned.

After the fire, I was allowed to learn to receive love offerings from *others,* from strangers, from friends and family who witnessed my process via social media. Truly amazing! Los Angeles friends would send clothes through the mail. A huge Christmas box arrived from a German sister who only knew me through Facebook. Each and every gift I received from a stranger felt like they and I had been friends forever. Women from all over California collected clothes, shoes, linens, bags, cosmetics, jewelry, and much more for many of us.

Everywhere I landed, friends wanted to help and shared however they could.

I never had a fundraiser before the GoFundMe page was set up for me by a friend and people shared so generously, with words, thoughts, time and money. Organizations from all over the country showed up and offered help. FEMA, the Federal Management Agency for disaster zones, supported survivors of the fire in ways I never knew existed in this country. Hundreds of containers rolled in. The local Lions Club opened its gate with what we called the "Disaster Shopping Center," all free for those who had lost everything. The Universe does not like a vacuum.

It was touching and at the same time overwhelming.

I have hardly ever asked for help in my life. I always figured situations out by myself, and sometimes I was simply too proud to "receive" or would have felt ashamed and even humiliated. I used to wonder if strings were attached when offered help, so I would say no.

My financial loss without any insurance is my responsibility to bear and of course that has not been covered by the gifts. And so what?

The experience of generosity, the outreach, the kindness of the heart, the love pouring out, and learning to receive friends' and strangers' gifts has changed me forever.

I called it "my year of Christmas"!

This is burned in my heart: Receiving is as much a virtue as giving. May the love flow both ways. May we all be givers and receivers."

* * *

WHAT AN INCREDIBLE STORY OF something good rising out of the ashes—in this case, literally. Joya's experience rendered her without and so she had to dive deep into the things that truly matter.

Why is giving so much easier for us than receiving, and why the discomfort when we are given to? There are many reasons. Here are a few:

- It feels vulnerable and falsely creates a less-than feeling for some of us. It can create a feeling in us of being "a taker."
- It can make us feel indebted and that we need to give back to the person who just gave to us.
- It can create fear, a "What does he want from me?" feeling, when someone gives to us.
- It can make us feel conceited or worry that we will appear to be entitled or "full of ourselves" if we simply say, "thank you," so we reject instead.
- We have been taught that it's "better to give than to receive" and therefore we are being "bad" if we receive.

I have literally seen people balk at going through doors that were being held open for them and opt to go through others instead, or go through an open door without acknowledging the person holding the door for them, as if to say, "I don't need your help."

I have also witnessed women with overflowing shopping carts and a couple of unhappy, squirming kids in the grocery store say, "No thanks" when asked if they need help taking their groceries to their car, when my guess is that would have been pretty helpful.

Perhaps part of the difficulty in receiving comes from the notion that if we receive, we are somehow indebted. But the truth is, everyone's job is to both give and receive as it comes up, organically, in life.

Giving is not tit for tat. We don't have to turn around and give automatically to the place from which we just received. In life, we have the obligation to be good at receiving rather than being a "taker." And we have the dual obligation to be good at both giving and receiving, not just giving. We are required to do both throughout life, like the tide, as needed.

We don't have to automatically compliment someone who compliments us, any more than we are required to reject the compliment. But hopefully, we can receive compliments as freely as we feel moved to give them. Ideally, we can offer and receive help as needed. We may have been taught "'Tis better to give than to receive," but if we take that axiom to an extreme in which only we give, we become poor at receiving. That robs others of the chance to give to us, which isn't a very nice thing to do. Remembering that blocking ourselves from receiving denies someone else their opportunity to give may make it easier for us to receive.

We may think, "If I don't do it myself, it won't be done correctly," and so we deny help instead of seeing how we can receive support for the things on our list.

This is where the airplane-oxygen analogy comes in handy. At the beginning of every flight, the flight attendant reminds us of the Federal Aviation Administration's guidelines: If there is a drop in cabin pressure or we are headed for a "water landing" (in other words, a crash!), you are to reach above and assemble your own oxygen mask first and take a few breaths before helping others. This is because we are no good to others if we are passed out cold—especially our loved ones. The same is true in life.

We are no good to anyone if we haven't taken a breath for ourselves.

A wife in my private couples' therapy practice once said that her husband "never" helped. He looked both hurt and surprised by this because he felt he did a lot for her. He reminded her of all the things he did for her all the time without her even asking: washing her car, walking the dogs and picking up after them—something he did because he knew she hated to do it—doing the grocery shopping and buying her items he knows she loves, and so on.

She said, "Yeah, that's true. But you never do the things I *want* you to do. For example, you never help with the dishes. I always have to do them by myself."

At this he looked truly annoyed and said firmly, "You don't let me! If I do them, you redo them! When I load the dishwasher, you unload it and redo it! Do you get how insulting that is? And worse, you jump up to do them after you finish your dinner even if I am still sitting at the table eating and leave me there alone. If you want help, *ask*. But don't do it yourself and claim I 'never' help!"

He was absolutely right. We can't do everything ourselves, without asking to receive, and then claim that no one ever helps us.

There is a reason that receiving is the first tool after getting clear in our desire: If you cannot receive, all the doing won't give you what you want. If you can't receive, all that you ask for in life will bump into your inability to receive and the Universe will go find someone else to give it to. It will find someone who *can* receive.

We teach people how to treat us. If you cannot receive, people think you're all right and don't need anything. So they stop offering. This is true whether it's about help, constructive feedback, or compliments. It will just *stop*.

There are many ways to exercise our receiving muscle. One is to begin by simply saying "thank you" to compliments, gifts, and help, or when a door is held open for you. Let the compliment or gesture soak in, fill you up, and make you feel warm. Be grateful for the words or action. Don't see compliments as flattery, someone "wanting something," or an indication that you have to return a compliment immediately.

Another way to exercise your receiving muscle is to create a gratitude journal. This helps you to count your blessings. Just as it's more fun to give to a person who receives our presents graciously and says thank you—and maybe even sends a thank-you note! — you become "more fun" for the Universe to give to when you accept with gratitude! Things, kindness, opportunities, peace, and so on, start to come your way.

A person who says thank you for their gift creates a warmer feeling in us than the person who doesn't acknowledge our gift. So too does the Universe like giving to a receptive heart. Keeping a gratitude journal, in which you write a list of at least three things you are grateful for every day, is like saying thank you to the Universe. You will find it brings in even more to be grateful for!

Learn to say "yes" to help. Simply work on learning to receive graciously, gracefully, and gratefully when offered. Being grateful for all you have and enjoy creates a feeling of fullness, which makes receiving easier.

Imagine the following scenario. You have a 9-to-5 job and just worked a hard day. You're ready to go home but still have to pick up your child from daycare and make dinner. You look at the clock and let out a frustrated sigh, groaning, "I still have to pick up my kid, sit in traffic, figure out something to make for dinner, and wash dishes. Same old grind."

Imagining that, how do you feel in your body? What tension, tiredness, or fatigue does it create? And what about mental fatigue? How does it reside in your psyche? Now imagine the same scenario, but this time you give a sigh of thanksgiving.

You say to yourself, "I am so grateful for my job in this economy. So grateful for the good that my work provides for others and the money it provides me. And now I get to go pick up Johnny, who owns my heart! Can't wait to see him! And then we get to share a meal together. I am so grateful for the plenitude of food that nourishes us and for the love in my home."

See how different that feels in your body and mind? Same scenario exactly. Just a different perception. This is called "reframing." Where can you reframe a current situation that is not imbued with gratitude and shift it?

Anything can be reframed with a perspective of gratitude. And life certainly gives us ample opportunity to do so. In every moment. In every moment, we have a choice. And, an opportunity to "reframe." How's that for a benevolent place? Life is continually giving us the opportunity to be grateful (or not).

Reframing simply means looking at how you label something and choosing to define it *differently*, changing how you see it. When you are judgmental of something, your thinking is limited and negative in that moment. See if you can take the opportunity to reframe it instead. For example, a child is crying in a restaurant and making a lot of noise and can't seem to be soothed. One thought might be, "What a spoiled brat. Wish people would leave their kids at home." But you could also change that to a more compassionate statement like, "That child looks hungry and tired. I feel for her."

Or a guy speeds past you on the freeway. You might think, "What a jerk. He thinks he is better than the rest of us." Or you can think, "He isn't driving safely." Period. Nothing personal. Your best friend or your partner is always late. You can think, "They are thoughtless and rude. Obviously I don't matter to them." Or, you can reframe it: "They have a different relationship to time than I do."

Another way to grow your receiving muscle is to pick up the coins you see on the sidewalk, stick them in your pocket, and say, "This is such a generous Universe! It supplies all my needs!" Or, "It's raining money!" In my Abundance Circles, when we work on the Receiving tool, I scatter a few coins on the floor before my students come in and don't mention them. Most of the time, the whole session passes and no one notices until I say, "Do you notice anything about the room tonight that is unusual?" Even then sometimes they don't see them. It's that way in life as well; there is an abundance of what we seek all around us and we don't even see it.

Abundance, in all its forms, wants to find you just as much as you want to find it.

Try replacing the word "get" with "receive" and see if you find that letting in the good begins to feel easier to you. "I am going to receive a cup of coffee." "I will ask to receive some help on this project." "I am going to receive a massage today." "I am going to receive my mail." "I am going to receive my child from school."

You get the idea.

You can also hold the intention of "receiving" in places where you would normally think of yourself as "giving" or "doing." When you are listening to your partner talk about his day, for example, you might say to yourself, "I am here to receive his story."

Ask your highest self to be open to receiving. Learn to identify yourself as a "good receiver" and allow blocks to receiving to be removed. Practicing in the small, everyday ways I've already mentioned will help exercise that muscle.

Try to be detached and allow what you want to come to you with grace, especially after you've gotten crystal clear in defining your desire and set the work piece into motion. Attachment can be a fearful state that shuts the door to receiving. Perhaps you have experienced this in your own life when you were in an interview for a job you really wanted, or when you really, *really* liked a boy or girl in high school and hoped they liked you back.

I remember once, during high school, pedaling my bike to my job. In the quiet of the ride, I had a quick and spontaneous thought that was something like, "Hmm! I haven't gone on a date in a while." Flipping that into a request. I just put out, without any attachment, "I'd like to go on some dates!" This was many years (decades, actually) before I knew anything about Law of Attraction or the fact that our thoughts create our reality. It was just a prayer. I said it and released it. The following week, I had dates on a couple of nights with different guys.

When my little rescue dog Faulkner runs away from home and I go searching for him in a panic around my neighborhood, I have several times asked to be shown which way to go and how to find him. When I do that, I'm led directly to where he is. When I forget and just run around frantically, searching willy-nilly, I'll be looking for a very long time, calling out his name and appearing a little nutty: "Faulkner! Faulkner! Where are you, Faulkner? Come here, Faulkner!" I have no luck until I remember to ask to be shown which way to go. Then, within mere minutes of asking for guidance, I find him. It just takes asking, trusting the request will be heard, and then letting go and being led to receive the help I seek.

Ask. Believe. Receive.

Letting go of the attachment is not about no longer caring. It means we trust that "this or something better" is on its way. It means we trust that we have been heard. It means we "let go of the how." Using that expression can even help in the process if you find you are perseverating on the outcome too much.

Think of it like ordering a pizza to be delivered. You don't order a pizza and then drive to the pizzeria and supervise the workers there as they make the pizza, put it into the right-sized box, load it into the car, and type your address into their GPS, and then follow them to your house, do you? No. You just *order the pizza*, knowing it will come. And so it is in life. You get crystal clear about what it is you want, you do the work necessary to produce it, and then you find the "sweet spot" of wanting it very much but being relaxed, knowing it's on its way.

You just expect that the delivery guy is coming.

Another way to build the receiving muscle is to say "Yes, *please!*" when things show up in your life, such an invitation to try new things or go somewhere. Practice the idea that if it's in your life, maybe you are meant to try it. For example, going out if you are invited, even if you are tired or think you won't like what you got invited to do or try. Then ask yourself, "What am I to receive from this experience?" What if you let life be the guide, just surrender, to its possibilities and let yourself receive life's rich bounty? What unseen gifts await when we allow ourselves to receive?

Look for ways to create the space to receive. You must let go of what no longer serves you and is cluttering your life. This allows for the good you seek to step in. Clutter can come in the literal form, or it might be a relationship, job, or city that isn't a fit for you. When you let go of what *isn't* in your highest good, you create the space for what *is* in your highest good. You can start with decluttering your closets and getting rid of clothes you haven't worn in over a year and donating them to charity. Then move on to other rooms or other places, like your bookshelves, your kitchen cabinets, under your bathroom sink, and so on. Look at other places you can declutter that may be less literal or tangible, like letting go of old resentments you have been carrying or lifestyle habits and relationships that feel toxic or unhealthy.

I am an absolute believer in giving. In fact, I begin my days with the question, "How can I be of service today?" Giving is good medicine for us and good for the receiver.

Just make sure you include yourself in the receiving.

I received an email from a past Abundance Circle member after her round of circles was over. She wrote that she was grateful for the Circle and specifically for learning about the Receiving tool. Having it changed her life.

For five years, she had been the emotional support for her best friend who had cancer and was with her through the dying process. Being both so intimately involved in giving to her friend and then in the subsequent "survivor's guilt," she had unconsciously taken on the habit of *not* receiving. It showed up in places unrelated to her friend and therefore she didn't notice that receiving for herself had stopped. However, she had stopped receiving from her husband and elsewhere. It was affecting her relationships; not receiving puts up blocks between us and the giver.

It blocks the path to intimacy because there is no path in, since "Intimacy" = "Into Me See." Not receiving obstructs closeness. In the session on receiving, she had an "aha" moment and made the connection that she had stopped receiving. She connected it directly with her experience with her friend and knew she needed to give to herself, too, by learning to receive.

How are *you* doing in the "receiving department"? Are you able to let in what comes your way, what life has to offer?

* * *

Your task is not to seek for love, but merely to
seek and find all the barriers within yourself
that you have built against it.

—Rumi

RECEIVING EXERCISES

1. Observe, don't judge, your relationship with receiving this week. What did it feel like when you were able and not able to receive?

2. Begin exercising your receiving muscle by accepting compliments graciously and without flinging them off of you. Receive help; ask for help. If someone opens a door for you, walk through it and thank them. Sounds simple, but our discomfort with receiving sometimes has us forget this! Don't dismiss kind words, gestures, or gifts. Sometimes we want to give or say something back immediately. Practice just receiving. You can give and receive organically.

3. Keep a gratitude journal. First thing in the morning, even before you check your phone, take out your journal and write at least three things you are grateful for. Go for depth over breadth in writing; express more of the deep gratitude you have for something rather than just listing a bunch of things.

A sentence or two expressing gratitude for several things you are deeply grateful for—from the mundane to profound—is a simple but powerful way to stay in gratitude. Before you go to bed at night or first thing in the morning, read your journal entry from the day before to anchor it in. Remaining in gratitude makes it easier to receive.

4. Adjust your language. Practice using the word "receive" where you would normally say "get" or "buy." Ask, "In what ways can I use the word 'receive' where I normally use 'get'?" What examples can you think of right now?

   When you pick up a book to read, go to your yoga class, attend a lecture, or listen to your partner, use this phrase before you begin: "I am here to receive." Then journal how this experience was different for you from times you previously said something to yourself like, "I had to be here" or "I am here to get" in similar scenarios.

5. Write down what you want to attract more of in your life using the present tense and the word "receiving": "I am receiving phenomenal clients who compensate me generously for utilizing my talents to their fullest potential and greatest good for all." If you are going on a job interview or are an actor going on an audition, say to yourself beforehand, "I am receiving this job/role today." Imagine how different your energy will be knowing you are going to receive something from someone rather than being in a position of needing something from them. That alone will have you feeling more comfortable and confident and less dependent and nervous, and you will therefore feel more at ease in front of them.

6. Create space for receiving. Declutter, declutter, declutter. Things, toxic relationships, stories, and resentments you carry and go over and over again—let that s#*t go. It isn't serving you any longer and is in fact holding you back. Time to release it.

CHAPTER 5
TOOL 3: SHADOW MATERIAL

Owning our story can be hard but not nearly as difficult
as spending our lives running from it… Only when
we're brave enough to explore the darkness will we
discover the infinite power of our light.

—Brené Brown

SHADOW MATERIAL REFERS TO THE parts of ourselves that are
repressed, denied, or underground. The Shadow is what Carl Jung
called "the person we would rather not be." It isn't necessarily "dark"
or negative; it is just hidden from the light of our awareness.

When we push down parts of ourselves that we deem unworthy,
we judge ourselves. We are also not being fully integrated or
authentic: By judging and rejecting these parts of ourselves, we
are not allowing them to be expressed. Much of our Shadow is
actually traits we were told were not nice or okay when we were
children—so we buried them.

How is this related to living more fully and abundantly? If we
have all the tools in the world for manifesting, they can only go so
far until they hit the wall of our Shadow. Since Shadow material is,
by definition, something hiding in the dark, we can try to have the

life of our dreams, but when we bump into our Shadow, we will be blocked and not know why.

To identify your Shadow material, start by thinking of the traits that bother you in other people. They are an indication of the parts of yourself that you have judged unworthy and undesirable. This is a good time to remember that old visual we were taught as children of pointing our finger at someone else and labeling them. When we do that, we have three fingers pointing back at us.

You see that annoying trait in others because you have it too (sorry!) and you have worked really hard to bury it. You are bothered because they are showing it to you. It is part of your Shadow.

A very common instance of Shadow material being revealed is when we hear of someone making a strident stance against a group of people for their lifestyle choices, only to find out they've been doing that very deed in private or have the very trait they have made their career condemning. Much like Shakespeare's line from *Hamlet*, "The lady doth protest too much, methinks," they are working extremely hard to hide the part of themselves they have deep shame about and call attention to in others. For something they are so bothered by, they certainly put a lot of protest, energy, focus, and light on it. They *are* the thing they denounce. If they came to terms with their Shadow, they would not point it out and condemn it in others.

We do not come into the world judging parts of ourselves or sending certain characteristics or attributes underground. It is only based on the reactions of people around us that we deem certain parts of ourselves not okay or unsafe.

Perhaps you danced around the living room as a little girl and your mother said you were "full of yourself," so you detest vanity. Or you were good at organizing play as a boy and your father said you were bossy, so you pushed those traits that smacked of "bossy" underground. To avoid being labeled, believing those traits must be bad, and to keep the approval of the adults taking care of you, you hid those traits even from yourself.

As children, we learn pretty quickly that our safety and well-being depend on grownups approving of us. On a primal, instinctual level, we are wired to know that if our parents reject us and kick us out of the nest, we will not survive. These are the people who provide us shelter, food, and warmth. We want them to love us, which in turn creates a sense of calm and security.

We would do all we can to avoid being called vain or bossy in order to feel safe, secured, and loved.

However, the positive side of vanity is confidence. The positive side of being "bossy" is being a good leader and organizer of groups. In this example, we must see what "bossy" has to teach us, what gifts it brings. In other words, we must stand in the place of not being defensive about it and not pushing it underground either. Because when our Shadow remains in the dark, it comes out in disastrous ways.

Amongst the traits we buried and hid in our Shadow is something very luminous and golden, much as a pearl comes from the uninvited grain of sand that irritates the oyster. Our Shadow contains a pearl of wisdom that will profoundly enrich our lives if we have the courage to dive for it.

As long as we see it as a negative and undesirable quality, however, it will remain the sand that irritates us. We will spend a great deal of our lives expending energy to deny it by reacting inappropriately when we express it. Or we'll try to cover it up in dysfunctional ways by compensating and sabotaging. We need to reframe our story about the part Shadow plays in our life, from "villain" to "teacher," and see what it has to teach us. We need to find the pearl it is holding for us.

How can we find the gifts of our Shadow?

We invite it in and look at it squarely.

If we were called "bossy" growing up and pushed anything remotely tied to that into Shadow, we detest "bossiness." We despise it in others and therefore might sugarcoat everything we say to people to avoid being seen as too bossy. Pushing our leadership underground may result in people doubting what we tell them. They may be able to sense that we are withholding things when we speak with them. Or they may feel we are afraid to lead. But if we embrace the good that "bossy" has to offer and learn to be direct and honest yet sensitive, people won't have to worry that when we tell them something, we don't really mean it. Or that we are thinking something but not saying it, thereby raising their anxiety a bit when they are around us. If we lead with confidence and feel safe and assured in our role, people will feel more comfortable knowing that we feel secure leading them and will in turn feel better under our guidance.

Or if, for example, we are afraid of expressing our anger because we believe it isn't "nice" and we stuff it every time we get triggered, we will eventually blow up in a way that is out of proportion. Neither we, nor the person who received our anger, will know where it came from.

That is the nature of Shadow. It strikes out. Better to integrate that part and use its positive side than to force it underground. *Either you own your Shadow, or it owns you.* In other words, what you resist, persists. As you know from your ability to manifest the things you do want in your life, putting your focus on something brings it in. The same law is true for pulling in what we do *not* want, and it takes a *lot* of energy to keep a quality or trait buried.

One of the tricky things about Shadow is that sometimes what bothers us when we see the *trait* in others shows up in them as *behavior* we would never engage in. Therefore we believe we don't have that trait and it remains completely unseen to us. Your Shadow trait may not show up in someone else as the same act. What bothers us in others could manifest in very different ways in our own life but still be our Shadow. Look at the personality trait you are being triggered by, not the specific behavior.

A member in one of my Abundance Circles said she is most triggered when people are mean to others. She said, "Because I just don't get that. I try to treat people with kindness at all times." Then she added after a reflective pause, "Except towards myself. I am not very kind to myself."

Voilà.

Shadow work looks past "anybody would feel angry about this like I do" because that is not the point. The gift for your own healing is to find what it brings up for *you* specifically. Why is it showing up in your life and what is it showing you about *yourself?*

ANGER IN SHADOW

MANY PEOPLE WITH ANGER IN their Shadow have either witnessed anger at its nastiest—often directed at them—or been told as children when they expressed it themselves that it wasn't "nice" and therefore interpreted that they weren't *allowed* to do so.

Learning to repress that emotion felt imperative, lest we behave like the angry, out-of-control people we saw, or be told that our feelings didn't matter or were wrong. Both are pretty rough options, so if our anger makes our caregivers mad, we learn to bury it. The trouble is, that can be taken to an extreme, such as not even feeling safe to express anger when we feel wronged, or in not setting proper boundaries with others. Or taking on too much so we don't make others mad when we say "no" to them. Or saying we are fine when we are actually upset. These are all examples of anger being in our Shadow.

Many people with anger in their Shadow fear that if they learn to express it, they will swing from being someone who represses his or her feelings to someone who rages as soon as they turn their light onto their hidden anger shadow. I hear from former anger stuffers in my practice all the time that they worry they will become ragers.

We don't swing from one extreme to the other when we do our Shadow work. That would just be responding from the opposite side of the same coin. If fear of being seen as an angry person means you don't set proper boundaries, when you look at the positive side of anger, you give yourself permission to do so in an adult, responsible way. You don't say "yes" when you mean "no," but you don't scream "no!" either.

Anger is a natural and understandable reaction and emotion to have when we feel wronged. Expressing that anger is a way of communicating our sense of injustice. If we don't express all of our emotions, ideally as constructively and responsibly as we can in every situation (that is the goal, anyway!), we are in essence saying to the little boy or girl inside of us that their feelings don't matter. In other words, we perpetuate the same message given in childhood: that our anger is "bad" and that our inner child needs to be quiet. Hopefully, when you think of it that way, it becomes clear how imperative it is to address our own Shadow material and give voice and expression to the child within.

A positive side of anger—and all shadow traits have a "light" or positive side—can be action, as when you let your anger out in positive, channeled ways, like turning toward and working for causes you care deeply about. Often being indignant is exactly the right response in a given situation. Maybe getting angry is the right response in some cases instead of turning a blind eye and inadvertently condoning improper behavior or actions.

SOFTNESS IN SHADOW

SOMETIMES IT ISN'T ANGER THAT gets driven into our Shadow, but the other extreme: showing our softer or feminine side or revealing the other emotions besides anger. This is especially true for boys, and it's unfair to them. They may have grown up hearing they were acting like a girl or a baby when they displayed hurt or sadness, which is also unfair to girls because it strongly implies that female is an inferior or weak thing to be. Or they have been told to "man up," which is not-so-subtle a code for "Stop whatever feeling you're having right now."

Girls too can get a similar message and be told not to be so sensitive when their feelings get hurt or they cry. They may have been told they were "too sensitive." In other words, "Push down your feelings." Rather than placing the focus on the person who caused the hurt feelings, the focus and responsibility is put on the girl to not let it bother her.

When people who grew up hearing it was wimpy to cry or express their feelings push hurt, vulnerability, and sadness into their Shadow, they can come across as lacking sensitivity when they see others emotionally hurt. Anger may be the only emotion they allow themselves to feel and they're impatient when anyone expresses something other than that. They in essence send a message: "Do what I do. Stuff that feeling down." They may see tears as a sign of weakness and be impatient with them.

Pushing tears down is not physically healthy, of course, and they need to be released. Acknowledging our sadness gets the feelings out of our body and helps in the healing process. Crying is not only *not* weak; it is beneficial.

The only way to get through the rough situations in our life is to go *through* them, not *around* them. We can't properly do that if we haven't acknowledged our Shadow. It's damaging to go through a grieving process with "It's not okay to cry" in our Shadow.

DISCOVERING WHAT COULD BE IN YOUR SHADOW

ANOTHER WAY TO BECOME ACQUAINTED with your Shadow is to look at a quality you like best in yourself. "Open-minded," maybe. Perhaps you even consider your open-mindedness your best quality and work hard to cultivate it. You are able to see new ideas and don't pre-judge people. Therefore, it is natural to think you aren't judgmental. What might be the opposite of open-minded? Perhaps rigid. Close-minded. Judgmental.

For example, maybe you are rigid and judgmental when you think about your loud and long-winded, opinionated uncle at Thanksgiving dinners. By judging him for being judgmental and rigid, maybe you yourself are being judgmental and rigid. So "rigid" and "judgmental" are your Shadow. It feels a lot better if we can come from a nonjudgmental and more open place, thereby inviting others by our example to come from openness too, rather than becoming what we don't like in them.

So your task is to learn how to bring the positive side of rigid and judgmental into your life. Where might rigidity be beneficial to you? Maybe in sticking to a particular exercise program or way of eating that is best for you. Or honoring your boundaries and not saying "yes" when you really mean "no." And perhaps the positive side of judgmental is "discerning." Perhaps, for example, you allow yourself to trust a feeling you immediately get when first meeting a person whose energy doesn't feel good to you.

* * *

OUR REACTION TO SITUATIONS GIVES our Shadows away. Here is a common context for people to get triggered: A person you're sharing the road with cuts you off while you're driving, and his dangerous driving infuriates you. You chase him down and weave in and out of traffic just so you can pull up next to him and give him the finger. "Boy, *that* really taught him!" Or you get in front of him to do the same thing to him that he did to you.

This behavior of others on the road is truly maddening. But let's break it down a bit.

When your Shadow pops up in reaction to a person's behavior or situation and you judge them for it and stay locked into that judgment, you are now on equal footing with that person or situation. And *that* means you now match them vibrationally. Is this what you really want? If they bother you so much, do you really want to be a match? Releasing your thoughts about it now raises your vibration again.

Better to reflect on why you were triggered and acknowledge your feelings. Maybe we felt interrupted and "cut off" as a child and were not listened to. Maybe you felt unseen, or you didn't feel safe. Or perhaps you were led to believe that your needs didn't matter and other people's needs were more important. When you get cut off by another driver or made to feel like your needs don't matter and people are not careful with them, you are highly triggered.

When we are aware of our triggers, we can acknowledge the angry child inside with something like, "It really bothers you when people treat you like your needs don't matter. That makes perfect sense." This can instantly have a calming effect. Much better than to react from your Shadow, which will actually reinforce and fortify the buried trait. When we react from Shadow, that place we work so hard to hide from the world, we expose that "horrible, nasty" side for ourselves and others to see, reinforcing that we *are* that kind of person and that the trait needs to be buried.

Sure, none of us likes getting cut off by other drivers. Nobody can tell you that that is a fun thing to have happen. But not everyone reacts with road rage either. Some can say to themselves, "That's really annoying. That guy is being a jerk." And then they are done. Or they say, "That guy is not driving safely, so I'm going to keep clear." You aren't saying that the other person's driving is all right with you. You aren't giving him a pass. Nor are you saying your feelings don't matter. You are saying the opposite; that the feelings *do* matter.

The way to process "big" feelings when they come up is, number one, to recognize what the feeling is (sadness, anger, frustration, hurt, mortification?). You do that first by checking in with yourself and listening to the answer. If you aren't sure what the feeling is, you can place a hand over your heart, be still, and say, "*I'm listening.*"

Second, acknowledge that feeling and the fact that the feeling matters.

Third, focus on the action you are going to take to tend to that feeling. It could be using your voice to say something to the person you feel hurt by or angry with. Or it could be that you do some journaling about your triggers, trying to access when they happened before and acknowledging that you are hearing the child inside. For example, you might say, "It feels really bad when you are yelled at and it's extra hard to take since your stepdad often yelled at you growing up" and see what comes up in your writing. But even just recognizing the hurt or anger and saying reassuring words to yourself is healing in itself.

The point is to look inward at the feelings coming up for a moment, rather than outward at the other person's behavior. Use the opportunity to discover what your Shadow is. The way to source it is to begin by asking how it *feels*.

* * *

DEEPAK CHOPRA REMINDS US THAT, "Our Shadow incites us to act out in ways we never imagined we could and to waste our vital energy on bad habits and repetitive behaviors." When we do our Shadow work and heal it, we can bring out its positive side. When it's recognized, our Shadow can become our greatest asset.

Of course, we live in duality. We are both judgmental and open-hearted, kind and spiteful, charitable and stingy. Stingy birthed the charitable in you. You might ask yourself, "Where in my life would it be good to be stingier?" Perhaps with your time? With your boundaries? Your resources? I have several clients who do very well financially and are constantly being hit up by relatives asking for large "loans" they do not pay back. They keep allowing it by saying yes. They tell me they don't want to but feel like they have to since they make more. If you deny that stinginess is part of your makeup and make it your Shadow, you may find you have difficulty saying no or setting boundaries because you think such moves are stingy. But it just might be that saying no more often would mean you had more time and resources to share and hence able to be more charitable. Owning up to all our parts, the traits we like and the ones we judge, only serves to make us more whole and well-rounded.

We feel we must fear the Shadow side of ourselves and the Shadow material in life because we have been conditioned to. We think not paying attention to what we perceive as bad will make it go away, but ignoring or repressing our Shadow material only intensifies it, leading to more pain and suffering. That material begins to control us rather than the other way around when, instead of excavating the gifts in the Shadow, we pretend we don't *have* Shadow.

Think about a person you dislike—living or dead, fictional or real, known to you personally or not—and write that name down. Then write three or four attributes they have. These will certainly be the traits that lead you to dislike them; they are mean, close-minded, selfish, judgmental, and so on.

Next, turn the proverbial pointing finger toward yourself. How or where do you own some of these same traits? They are your Shadow. How can you flip these qualities into positives and find their gifts? How do the positive sides of these traits serve you? How might they become your greatest assets?

Author Jacob Nordby writes, "Every pain, addiction, anguish, longing, depression, anger or fear is an orphaned part of us seeking joy, some disowned shadow wanting to return to the light and home of ourselves." It's not about getting rid of certain aspects of ourselves, but finding the positive side of these aspects.

A former client I will call Frederick was a highly successful businessman who worked sixty hours a week. He was always on the phone with work, even when at home or on vacation with his wife. He took many business trips to incredible places all over the world—with only other work people there. His wife was not invited. When they were together, he almost always only talked about his work. He was, in essence, having an affair with his job. His wife ended up having an affair of her own. With the neighbor.

Yes, Frederick's job paid for a wonderful life and his wife got to stay at home with their baby, a choice they both felt good about when they made it. He thought he was providing and that she should be happy. But she was lonely. And depressed. And felt ignored. The relationship had no "light" on it.

After their divorce, he realized that his Shadow included feeling worthless. As a child, he was made to feel he wasn't okay unless he excelled. He was highly criticized and felt like he wasn't "good enough" in his parent's eyes. His job provided him with esteem, respect, and recognition from others, a little fame, and a boatload of money. He was in overdrive to compensate for his Shadow. And it cost him his marriage.

Fortunately, he learned that this was not who he wanted to be in life. He wanted to be a whole person in the world, not a machine, so he tended to the other aspects of his life: emotional, psychical, mental, and spiritual. He learned there was more to him than what he could provide. He remembered that his value lies in just being who he is.

In one Abundance Circles group, there was a woman whose father drove an hour each way to and from work every day when she was a little girl and who had been very tight with the money he worked so hard for. The six children were each allowed one pair of shoes a year. As a child, this woman heard the arguments about money and how her father had to work so hard to provide for his family but still there was never enough. He always seemed put out by this fact.

She had a very hard time making a substantial amount of money in her adult life or asking her past boyfriends and husband for anything. In speaking about Shadow, she linked her father's view of money being tight—never enough—with the story she carried that she didn't deserve to have things into her adult life. When she made that connection, she had a deep epiphany, an "aha!" and flipped that belief around.

This is her story:

When I was a little girl, around ten, I remember my dad yelling to all six of us in the house, "Who got new shoes this month?!" My dad used to drag a box of bills down the hallway once a month to sit at the dining table and pay them. We hated those days and would hide. This particular time, it was me who got a pair of shoes. My feet had grown. My mom took me shopping and allowed me to pick out black patent leather shoes with black and white shoelaces. My dad made me bring the new shoes out and told my mom to return them. My three sisters laughed at me because I chose fancy shoes.

As an adult, when I made money, I would buy shoes. Not designer shoes, but nice shoes on sale. At one time, the most I had was fifty pairs. My favorites were patent leather in black, pink, red, and sparkly silver. I have since simplified and I am down to twenty pairs and six of those are athletic shoes!

Doing Shadow work heals our inner child. Because the things you put in your Shadow were traits or feelings you learned were "bad" when you were a child, validation of all of your child feelings as true for you creates safety for you to be more fully yourself. In essence, you become the perfect parent for your inner child. Listen to her. Speak to her with compassion. Be mindful of your self-talk.

Carl Jung asked, "Would you rather be good or whole?" Embracing our Shadow creates wholeness in ourselves and makes us more authentic. It is liberating to embrace *all* of our qualities and use each trait in its kindest, highest form. In that way, we are not only being true to who we are but also bringing more gifts to the world. Recognizing our Shadow means we don't have to judge parts of ourselves as deficient or "bad" anymore. It means we can come home to all we were created to be—a "homecoming" to our full and authentic self.

* * *

FACING OUR SHADOW TAKES RIGOROUS honesty, bravery, and deep compassion. Jung also said, "Shadow work is the path of the heart warrior." It's true. It is for the brave.

The consequence of *not* doing our Shadow work is a life that is less authentic, happy, and full. If we don't do the work, we will live a life of judgment toward ourselves and others, be continually triggered, go around projecting our Shadow onto others, and generally feel more negative and limited. Our dreams will remain unfulfilled because we will be too afraid to act on them.

Until we feel authentic compassion for each and every aspect of ourselves, we will continue to draw forth people and events that will mirror the negative feelings we have about ourselves. Until we take back our power and forgive ourselves for being human, we will attract people who push our buttons and reactivate our emotional wounds. And until we find the courage to love ourselves completely, we will never truly be able to experience the love from those around us.

Shadow work is the tool that Abundance Circle participants are least likely to have heard of before, and lively (albeit sometimes arduous) discussions ensue when we address it. Because the material is new as a concept and brings up elusive, unknown parts of us, it requires two sessions instead of one in the Abundance Circle groups.

When it's left buried deep within our unconscious, away from the light of awareness, Shadow has a kind of invisible hold on us that dictates who we show up as, who we are drawn to and choose as partners, how we think and feel, the level of success we allow ourselves, and what we judge and dismiss. The Shadow material can only control us if it is kept in the dark.

Imagine, instead, bringing it into the light and excavating powerfully beautiful, exquisite gems like compassion, forgiveness, brilliance, and the capacity to live more authentically and broadly. Imagine basking in that kind of assuredness and totality. Imagine being that clear when your intuition tells you something. Imagine being that bold when you have a message to share with the world. Imagine being that nonjudgmental when people make choices you wouldn't. Imagine loving yourself unconditionally because you know all parts of yourself are gifts. Imagine not hiding!

Look out, world! Beep! Beep! Get out of my way!

SHADOW EXERCISES

HOW CAN YOU BENEFIT TODAY from observing, not judging, your Shadow material? Journal about it. You may also want to consider doing artwork around the topic.

SHADOW-FINDING EXERCISE

HERE IS ANOTHER WAY TO discover what is in your Shadow. It's a flash journal exercise.

1. Look at the quality you love most about yourself. What's the *first* thing you think of?
2. Write it down.
3. Now, what do you think is the negative opposite of that trait?
4. Write it down. That is your Shadow!

5. What are some positive attributes of the quality you wrote is your Shadow? How might these traits serve you well when integrated into your life?

When we discover our Shadow side and bring it to light, we allow its positive traits to shine, which is an enormous part of accepting ourselves.

We all have valuable characteristics in our Shadow.

CHAPTER 6
TOOL 4: "I AM" STATEMENTS

THE NEXT TOOL IS AN ancient and powerful one. It is comprised of the two most influential words in our language when spoken together: I AM.

Think about how powerful they are. Everything you attach to these words, you become. Everything you say after these two words is a declaration to the world. Everything you say after "I AM" defines you. "I am bad at this." I am beautiful." "I am joyous." "I am old." "I am a writer." "I am a burden." "I am not wanted." "I am compassionate." "I am abundant."

I AM is an affirmation every time you say it.

I AM is a pure statement of *creation*.

Whatever follows I AM gets created in the outer world.

Words we attach to our I AMs become our unconscious voice as well, because they become hardwired in our brain as "truth." We say I AM statements throughout the day and aren't even aware of many of them. And because we draw into our external world what we create internally, we end up getting "proof" of our I AMs.

When you become aware of the I AMs you say, you will see how I AMs have the force to ignite, empower, and embolden you, or the weight to limit you. Everything you say after I AM seems to find its way to you.

All religions and spiritual paths are based on the I AM. In Judeo-Christian scripture, it appears numerous times in both the Old and New Testament and appears in Eastern scriptures as well.

In the Old Testament, it is the way God revealed Himself to Moses when asked who was speaking to him through the burning bush: "I AM THAT I AM." In other words, simply, I AM *this*.

In the New Testament, Jesus is quoted as making I AM statements seven times in the book of John to explain who he is.

In the Hindu Vedic traditions, I AM is known as Brahma. Brahma, the creator god of Hinduism, is otherwise known as "I AM the Ultimate" and used to explain the unity of all, both micro- and macrocosmic. The South Indian Hindu sage Ramana Maharshi mentions that of all the definitions of God, "None is indeed so well put as the biblical statement 'I AM THAT I AM.'"

Buddhists call it the Dharmakaya. The Dharmakaya is the Absolute, the essence of the Universe, and the unity of everyone and everything.

This incredibly short religious history lesson shows that if God revealed Him/Herself in that way, the words "I AM" themselves are sacred and deserve to be said from a sacred space. Therefore, let everything you say after I AM be said from your highest place. As often as possible, use kindness, positivity, and connectivity after these words.

Notice, "I AM" is in the present tense. It isn't "I hope to be." It isn't "I used to be." It is something known to you right now and as truth. Whatever you want more of in your life, follow that desire with an "I AM." Say it with feeling, as if you feel it to be true down to your bones, whether or not you already do.

If you want more abundance, say, "I AM abundant." If it's good health you seek, say, "I AM healthy and strong."

Be careful of limiting or derogatory remarks. If you don't understand a concept or the latest gadget, be mindful and avoid saying, "I am so old!" If you miss a turn you meant to take while driving or don't get a hundred percent on a test, don't say "I am so stupid!"—even if you are joking when you say it. Your mind doesn't know the difference between fact and fiction, nor between seriousness and joking, so your words alone give the signal to your consciousness, not the interpretation of those words.

I had a young woman client who was often involved in car accidents, on the receiving end. She'd be stopped at a red light and someone behind her would not stop and slam into her. Or she'd be in a parking lot, going slowly, and someone would blindside her. It happened with uncanny frequency. And as is the pattern of the Universe trying to call our attention to what we need to look at, the accidents got bigger and more serious as their number grew. There was some message she wasn't hearing, some clue she wasn't getting.

This is a person who used to say, "Well, with *my* luck..." followed by some arbitrary awful thing when someone said, "Have a good week!" or "See you tomorrow!" Why is it we never hear people place a positive scenario after "With my luck...!"? Like, "Well, with *my* luck, I'll probably win the lottery!"

After her appointment with me one day, I said, "Have a great week!" as she was leaving, and she again said something that began with, "Well, with my luck…", alluding to something horrible that would probably happen between now and when we met next the following week.

I shared my observation that she did that and was actually putting out negative orders to the Universe with these comments. In later sessions, we looked at why she said them and also at the "why" beneath all the blindsiding and rear-ending. She realized that she thought of herself as a victim and did not feel safe. She never knew when she might be "blindsided" by life and thrown off her game plan.

After she became aware of it, the healing of that wound could begin. Awareness is always the first step in changing something. We worked on healing around that story, including addressing where it had come from, and she changed her thoughts about it. In essence, her therapy consisted of re-parenting the parts of herself that did not feel protected or connected. She also realized she led a pretty privileged, healthy, happy, and full life and stopped declaring herself unlucky by learning to be more mindful, grateful, and present in the moment.

She was anxious for the car accidents to stop and certainly didn't want them to get any worse. She made a concerted effort to watch her I AMs. She began to see herself as safe and protected, and her life as being on track. She practiced feeling fortunate and grateful for her life and not like a victim. It was seven years ago that she made the shift and she hasn't had an accident since.

Think of I AMs as placing an order to the Universe. Don't order what you don't want.

You came into the world a perfect little being, with a place in the tapestry that is this planet. You were the perfect "you." You didn't say as a baby, "It's 3:00 a.m. Who am I to cry for milk at this hour?" Or, "I am in a public place. It's best I not shriek with glee at the top of my voice." You came in packaged exactly right, and in full awareness of your I AMs.

You came in with no concept of Shadow material, or that some parts of yourself were "good" and others "bad." You had a voice and you used it.

Exploring your Shadow material and healing it, knowing your I AMs, and embracing that adorable, amazing self you came in as, and still are, are all steps on your path and journey of homecoming to your authentic self.

Our inner relationship fractures when we get messages from the outside world or tell ourselves stories from our experiences. We lose sight of our true essence. We compare ourselves to others and either feel inferior and "less than" or "better than" others instead of remembering we are all just variant and meaningful iterations of the same human tribe, each with beautiful and unique offerings.

I like thinking of life as a table with four legs. If one of those legs is cut shorter than the others, the table will be out of balance. The four legs consist of our Emotional, Physical, Mental, and Spiritual lives. Remember "Frederick," my client in the Shadow chapter who tended to only one part of his life—his work—and it cost him his marriage? When he shifted his focus to include attention to all four legs of the table, it changed his life. Each of those places needs tending and requires us to receive attention and energy in order to feed them. When life feels out of balance, ask yourself, "Where am I not receiving?" Not, "What do I need to *do?*" Remember, you are a human being, not a "human doing."

You can apply I AM statements to the "four legs" of your being. Examples will follow each "leg."

Your emotional life has to do with watching your thinking and responses, and how you react to others and situations. It means paying attention to what is welling up in you and what you suppress, how strongly you feel about something, and honoring those emotions. It is looking at your wounds as they arise so that they can be addressed and healed. It's about always trying to grow as a person. It's watching your self-talk, not judging yourself, and using the mistakes of your life to try and do better.

Some examples are: I AM calm. I AM kind. I AM empowered.

Your physical life has to do with your body and health, and treating and tending to your body as though it were a temple. Because it is. It's about being mindful of the foods you eat and getting enough exercise, fresh air, rest, and sleep. It's about saying kind things to yourself about your body and not judging it.

Some examples are: I AM strong. I AM healthy. I AM beautiful.

Your mental life has to do with acuity, brain stimulation, learning, staying updated on current issues, and developing new ideas. Tending to this leg of the table could include studying, learning a new language, starting a new hobby, or opening yourself up to other new ideas.

Some examples are: I AM bright. I AM a foreign language ninja! I AM open-minded.

Your spiritual life may or may not include religion. Your spiritual life has to do with finding your purpose, remembering your part in the whole, feeling connected to and respecting other people and all life, having quiet time and reflection, and being in nature. It is about considering the larger Universe—the greater truths of our needs, thoughts, desires, and the needs, thoughts, and desires of others. Appreciation and gratitude are an important piece of the spiritual. I AM connected. I AM bliss. I AM compassion.

What I AMs could you apply to your life in these categories?

One Abundance Circle client of mine, who had grown up being told she was ugly by her mom, sent me a text with a photo of her bathroom mirror. She had written all over it in bright red lipstick, "I AM BEAUTIFUL! I AM BEAUTIFUL! I AM BEAUTIFUL!"

* * *

THERE IS A POPULAR YOUTUBE video in which a photographer captured what happens when people are told they are beautiful. The then-eighteen-year-old high school student Shea Glover conducted an independent social experiment. She wrote, "I want to clarify that my intentions were not to get a reaction out of people. I was simply filming beauty, and this is the result." She posed people in front of her camera and then told them, "I'm taking pictures of things I find beautiful." She posted photos of each subject before and after this comment.

The photographs are stunning in their contrast. There is so much light in the faces of the subjects after Shea tells them they are beautiful. In truth, they appear more beautiful to us, the viewers, after they are told this. Shea holds a beautifully accurate and loving metaphoric mirror up to her subjects and they see their own beauty reflected in it.

The wonderful thing is, our mind does not distinguish between our telling ourselves something and hearing it from an outside source! You are free to tell yourself you are beautiful—or powerful, incredible, amazing, successful, generous, *fabulous!*, or whatever you want—at any time of the day, as often as you wish, and no one is going to label you "full of yourself" or "arrogant," or ask, "Who do you think you are?"

You are free to "I AM..." to your heart's content.

In my work with private clients or in Abundance Circles, I have seen people turn their limiting or defeating thoughts about themselves around, and therefore change the world around them, giving themselves proof of the positive opposite and changing their beliefs entirely.

For example, if you grew up with a learning handicap or in the shadow of an extremely gifted older sibling, you may have suffered under the weight of the thought that you were "not smart."

Or perhaps you grew up conscious of the fact that money was always scarce; maybe you heard the expression "Money doesn't grow on trees," or that it was the root of all evil. Or maybe you didn't have as many things as the other children in your class at school. Or you may have heard your parents arguing over the money they spent on you. Then you might have grown up with the belief that money is always scarce or that you are "broke" or "don't deserve." Without intending to, you might say, "I can't. I don't have any money," when a friend invites you out. Or you might say something like, "I wish I could take that trip, but I am too broke right now" (guilty as charged). Or, "I can't spend that kind of money on something just for myself."

It's one thing to say, "I am choosing not to spend money on that right now," and quite another to say, "I am always too broke to do anything fun." These "there isn't enough for me" thoughts become your "I AM" beliefs. They become "I AM not worthy" statements. Every time you think a statement like this, you anchor it in more deeply, like the needle on a record player going over and over the same track on an old LP, deepening the groove, driving the belief deeper into your unconscious.

Your thoughts and statements become your truth and you will see proof of your truth everywhere. Think of it like putting on glasses with your belief engraved on the lenses and seeing the world only through those glasses. Everything you look at has your core beliefs superimposed on it.

What do you imagine would happen if you were to flip thoughts about being broke or unworthy with I AM statements like "I have plenty," "I AM abundant!" and "I AM worthy!"? You can turn around your negative and limiting beliefs by noticing your negative I AMs and replacing them with positive ones.

The only person in charge of you is you. The only person who can program your I AMs is you. So choose carefully and consciously.

Some examples of I AM statements are:

"I AM enough." A quick "I AM enough" internet search brings up hundreds of hits on Pinterest, Facebook, various "I AM enough" blogs and campaigns, and the accompanying "I AM enough" T-shirts and bracelets for sale. A lot of people are searching for ways to remember that they are already enough.

Other I AM statements to consider:

"I AM beautiful." I suggest you do this every time you spritz your astringent or splash your aftershave on your face!

"I AM open and receptive to all the wealth life offers me."

"I AM open and receptive to meeting my life partner."

"I AM healthy, strong, and fit."

"I AM a money magnet."

"I AM kind, I AM happy, I AM magnificent!"

"I AM grateful for all I have."

"I AM present, aware, and conscious."

"I AM inspired."

Your I AMs can also remind you of who you really are and the traits you want to emphasize; in other words, the you that you came in as.

"I AM compassionate. I AM trusting. I AM intuitive. I AM loyal. I AM generous. I AM kind. I AM artistic. I AM strong…"

You create your life with your I AMs.

When you affirm your I AMs and state them often and with feeling, you begin to reconnect to that highest, truest part of yourself that is your beauty, your wisdom, your kindness, your light. Your strength. Your compassion.

And when you embody these truths, watch what happens in your life. People respond to what you believe to be true about yourself as well.

Watch your I AMs carefully. If you say, "I AM a victim," "I AM unattractive," or "I AM boring," people will let you know they agree with you.

And if you say, "I AM beautiful," "I AM a beacon of light," "I AM warm, approachable, and friendly," "I AM artistic and talented," and "I AM a leader and highly influential," people will see it too and let you know they agree with you.

Write your list of I AMs from remembrance of the truth about who you are, not the wounded self or the part that may be a mask or an old "story" about you that you learned from the world.

Write from the you who existed before you felt it better to hide or deflect attention from some of your parts. Write those cute little kid *I AMs*! and affirm them often and with gusto. You will draw people and situations into your life that validate those traits. Want to know why?

Because they are true and really you.

I AM EXERCISES

1. Observe, don't judge, the thoughts you have throughout the day that begin with "I AM." Are they kind? Are they true? Do they restrict and limit you? Or do they celebrate you? When you forget to do something or can't figure something out, is your very first thought "I am so stupid," or "I am so forgetful"? Or do you merely say, "Oops! Forgot to do that thing!"?

2. Think of three people you admire, alive or passed, real or fictional, known or unknown to you. Get out your journal and write down several traits for each of them. An example might be Atticus Finch from *To Kill a Mockingbird*. Some of his traits are:

- Honesty
- Deep integrity
- Loyalty to his truth
- Steadfastness
- Kindness
- Patience
- Compassion
- Passion

Look at that list of attributes.

You know what? Those are your I AMs! You wouldn't see those traits in others and be attracted to them if you didn't have them yourself.

Take some Post-it notes, notecards, or larger pieces of tagboard and place these I AMs around the house, on your bathroom mirror, your car dashboard, the refrigerator. Let them sink in.

Embody your I AMs!

3. Become conscious of using I AMs and immediately correct the negative ones you think or utter. Quickly flip them into positives, even if you don't believe them in that moment. Remember, the mind doesn't know the difference between fact and fiction. If you say or think it, the mind believes it. "I AM fat" gets flipped to "I AM fit" and "I AM so stupid!" gets flipped to "I AM so wise!" (Or smart, intelligent, bright, or capable. Whatever you feel drawn to say!)

4. Remember to say, "I AM beautiful" (or "loving," or whatever feels good for you) when you spritz your face after washing it or splash it with aftershave!

CHAPTER 7
TOOL 5: LOVE VERSUS FEAR

You need power only when you want to
do something harmful, otherwise love is
enough to get everything done.

—Charlie Chaplin

THE TRUE OPPOSITE OF LOVE is not hate. It is fear. Love and fear
are the two fundamental human emotions. All others are just
subcategorical elements of these two. Where there is love, we may
have joy, peace, contentment, serenity, and forgiveness. On the flip
side, fear creates anxiety, sadness, depression, fatigue, judgment,
guilt, and so on.

People and nations will kill others out of extreme fear.

And sometimes people will die for someone they love.

Where there is love, fear cannot survive, and where there is fear,
love cannot survive.

Love is our natural state. It's how we came packaged. Babies are
bundles of pure love. There is no such thing as a hateful baby. And
if their environments are safe and their needs are met, they are not
fearful by nature. They only feel fear when something frightening
or threatening happens *outside* of themselves.

As you apply the tools in this book and your life shifts and the desires that previously eluded you start manifesting in your life, it can feel a little foreign. Fear can step in. Although we are finally manifesting the life we dared dream of, our old Shadow material can show up and we can feel afraid. We can actually feel afraid when we begin to get what we want! Old limiting beliefs about us not deserving what we receive rear their heads. We may fear that it will all be taken away or that we bit off more than we can chew. We might think, "New levels, new devils," meaning this new way of being creates its own set of obstacles and challenges. There is a German proverb that says, "Fear makes the wolf bigger than he is." Why do we believe we don't deserve? Why does fear raise its head?

It's trying to protect us.

If we got messages, growing up, that we were full of ourselves; or that the world is a scary place and people are out to get us; or that we weren't smart enough, beautiful enough, or good enough; or that we were too much, unlovable, or in the way, it makes sense that it would be scary for us to show up fully. Even people from loving, supportive homes can have wounds or fears about showing up. If you received a belief that you were only all right when you were achieving, it could be difficult to show up mightily because fear might say, "What if this time you fail? What if your success is tied to your self-worth? Maybe if you don't succeed, it's going to feel really, really bad." Fear steps in and tells us not to even try. In the process, we hold back, play smaller, don't take risks, and withhold love, all in the hope of not getting hurt again.

Wounds set in when painful events like moving often as a child, abandonment, hurtful comments or being bullied happen. And those wounds get anchored in when we tell ourselves a story about those events in our lives. It is not the event itself so much as it is the meaning that gets attached to it that anchors in wounds. As an example, getting a poor grade on a paper you worked hard on as a child isn't the issue, per se. It is what you told yourself about yourself when it happened that is the issue.

For example, if you felt unheard as a child, it may have led to the development of a core belief that no one wants to listen to you and that you have nothing important to say. Imagine if that is your belief and you are asked to present something onstage to an audience. Yikes! What is fear going to say to you? It's going to say something like, "Are you sure you can do this? Are you sure they want to listen to you? Do you have anything of value to add?"

That certainly doesn't boost confidence.

Fear is trying to say to us, "It could be dangerous to step out and be seen by others. Maybe you should just play small. Remember that time in the past when you tried this and that scary thing happened? Yeah. Well, that didn't work out very well, did it? Maybe you should just say no to doing *that* again. Maybe you should play smaller."

This is why people who win the lottery or inherit a lot of money often find themselves at their previous income level not so long afterward. We must do our inner work in order to both attract what we say we want in life and to keep it.

That's where the Love Versus Fear tool comes in.

* * *

Fear and love can never be experienced at the same time. It is always our choice as to which of these emotions we want.

—Gerald G. Jampolsky

FEAR SHOWS UP IN OUR lives because we believe that, if we plan ahead for all the bad things we are so sure will happen, we will be prepared and therefore avoid being blindsided. But the trouble with this kind of thinking is that it creates inertia and anxiety. It also floods our bodies with stress hormones. If we do this enough, it creates dis-ease -and sometimes disease. Looking at all the things that can go wrong doesn't help us move forward with eyes wide open for the possible pitfalls. Instead, it creates blocks and leaves us unsure of what to do.

Fear also steps in when we are out of the present moment. Sometimes we are legitimately fearful because a dangerous or frightening event is happening at that moment. The majority of the time, though, fear rears its head because we are out of the present, having catapulted ourselves into the future and imagined all kinds of monsters there. Bad, tragic things that will never take place are given a lot of time, space, and energy even though they won't even happen.

There is an acronym for FEAR: **F**alse **E**vidence **A**ppearing **R**eal. As we imagine the thing we are worried about, that thing seems really real, and our brain and body even register it as actually happening! But it isn't. It isn't real. It just feels like it is.

When you find yourself there, leave. Why would you want something taking up so much space in your head and firing off all kinds of chemicals into your body if there is no danger around? Come back to now. Try replacing your fear with *curiosity* instead. The future is pregnant with marvelous possibilities. You are worrying about something bad that will probably never happen instead of swimming in the glorious possibilities of what could be! Take a breath and say to yourself, "That isn't even happening. Why am I letting something take up so much space in my brain without charging it rent?"

* * *

And the day came when the risk to remain tight in a
bud was more painful than the risk it took to blossom.

—Anais Nin

HOW DO YOU KNOW THE difference between love and fear when
faced with making a choice? Choosing love expands you. Choosing
fear constricts you. You will know which of the two you are choosing
by how your body feels. You can feel in your body that choosing love
feels light and right, while choosing fear feels suffocating, confining,
and tight. A fear-based choice will feel like it comes from your head
and thoughts. You might feel resigned after making a decision based
on fear, rather than relieved and excited. When your choice comes
from your heart, it comes from love.

You will also know by the words you say to yourself. When you
choose fear, you say things like, "I am afraid if I don't, then…" or
"I worry that…"

An example of fear is the college student who is passionate
about English literature but majors in something she can't stand
for four years because she thinks it will guarantee her a job when
she graduates.

Literature was her saving grace as a child and young adult. Its
mystery, beauty, and intrigue bring immense value to her life. It takes
her "away" when she wants to escape and enriches her imagination.
Literature informs the way she sees the world and expands her
viewpoints. She identifies with some of the heroines and takes
away valuable lessons. She wants to study it in depth and hopes to
impart her love to a younger generation.

But her parents dissuade her and say, "What are you going to do? Open an English store when you get out?" They bring up the cost of her tuition and how she is "wasting" it on something that won't provide for her when she gets out of school. She is afraid they are right that she won't get a job when she graduates if she majors in English lit, or afraid they will be mad at her if she sticks with it. She majors in accounting instead and is bored out of her mind.

Another example is the woman who marries a man she doesn't love or who stays with an abusive husband because she thinks she could never find anyone else.

I had a twenty-something client who was with a hot-tempered guy who put her down constantly. The way he spoke to her was absurd. He openly cheated on her and denied it when caught with proof like romantic texts to other girls on his phone. He didn't have a job and she paid for everything. They moved in with her parents and he didn't contribute to the household chores or expenses. He went out every Friday night with his friends and wouldn't let her join him. He was constantly insulting and verbally abusive to her. The longer the verbal abuse went on, the worse it got because she wasn't backing herself up: an example of the clues "getting bigger" on the outside to get our attention.

But when I asked why she stayed with him, she said, "Because I am afraid of being alone." Can you hear the fear-based decision in that? Love would say, "I love myself too much to be in this and I would rather be alone than with someone who treats me this way." And leaving him would rewrite her story of it being okay to be mistreated because her childhood also contained molestation and verbal abuse. By staying, she was perpetuating the idea that it was okay to be treated like that and that she was powerless.

I am happy to add that as she looked at the stories she told herself based on the demeaning abuse she received growing up, she was able to see that she deserved more—*way* more. She grew confident, went on to get a master's degree in psychology, and is in a new relationship with a man who treats her well. Together they had a baby and bought a new home.

Unnecessary fear can show up in parenting or romantic relationships and smother the receiver of our fear. For example, we might hover very anxiously over our child as he learns to walk or ride a bike and create anxiety in him. Or we may try to control the friends our child plays with rather than letting her learn to deal with all kinds of people. We might feel anxious as she transitions from the roots to wings stage and begins to move away from us (as children are supposed to do if we have done a good job of parenting) and try to rein her back in. Conversely, rather than hovering, we can be too fearful of setting appropriate boundaries with our kids if we are afraid they won't like us or will get mad at us as a result. None of these behaviors create the desired outcome and all come from our own fear.

In romantic relationships, I have seen people destroy good relationships because they were fearful their partner was going to leave them. Either they were overly clingy and smothering or started frequent and silly fights, unconsciously provoking the other to leave since they "knew" they were going to leave anyway. This is particularly true of people who have abandonment in their history.

A pleasant side effect of living life from a place of love as often as possible is that it *feels* good! You notice the good that is around you more. You feel less thrown when the unexpected shows up in your life. People will be drawn to you without their really knowing why, and because like attracts like, when you are pleasant, kind, thoughtful, and loving, you will attract the same.

The passion you have in your heart is there for a reason and it's your job to cultivate and share that passion. When you come from love, you will be amazed how the Universe conspires to open doors for you. Consider the expression, "Don't push the river. It runs by itself." When you come from fear, you are pushing the river.

When we chose love, whether we are choosing something for ourselves or for another, the outcome is good. When we make a choice from fear, that may not be true, even if, for a brief period, it feels like the right choice. Because love is a higher frequency than fear, it leads to the right decision.

Connie is the yoga instructor in L.A. I mentioned at the beginning of the book who was financially devastated if she got a parking ticket and the money had to come out of her meager rent and food budget. Despite her lack of funds, she enrolled in a round of Abundance Circles because she intuitively knew that it would provide her with tools she needed to get out of the stuck place she was in. It was bold and wise to trust that inner wisdom.

What Connie most deeply wanted was to travel, do yoga, which she loves, immerse herself in another culture, and teach. Those four things were what brought her the most joy in life and what set her soul on fire. Although newly single, deeply in debt, and barely able to pay living expenses with a bartending job and a couple of yoga students, her plan was to try and work, pay off her debt, and *then* follow her heart's desire to do yoga and teach in another country. At the pace she was going, that would have taken decades; she wasn't earning enough to pay off any debt, let alone save.

Sometimes Connie felt the Abundance Circles tools were good in theory, trusted them, and saw them working for the other women in her group who were having huge and positive shifts even before the round she was in was over. But she was not convinced they would work for her, given her circumstances. She could see no way to make her dream a reality.

She could not imagine "A way out of no way."

While she was bartending part-time and teaching yoga to a couple of students, staying with friends and feeling like a nomad, her desire to do yoga and teach abroad was strong. But the voice in her head would tell her that this was irresponsible, even impossible— how would she ever get the money to fly abroad and how would she support herself when she got there? She had debt to pay off, the couple yoga students she felt accountable to, and teachers she felt connected with. It was the "grown-up" thing to do, sticking with a job even if she didn't like it, and it felt on track—although she didn't know where she was going. To leave what she knew, even though she hated it, for something unknown—in a foreign country, yet—felt extremely scary. She didn't know where to start anyway.

However, continuing to stay in the L.A life felt like living as a smaller version of herself. She was playing small and her gifts needed to reach more people. In addition, she heard a call and could not ignore it.

So Connie spent time trying to pay attention to and honor both the places that coexisted in her at the time. She held the vision of the thing she truly desired in her heart while also being present as she continued to work her part-time job to earn money and do her yoga, grateful in every moment for whatever she was doing right then and for what she had. In the time before she made a decision, she said she "kept honoring both sides and asking the Universe to open the doors that were meant for me: If leaving would serve a higher purpose, then show me the way, allow me to go. And if staying was where I was most needed to be, then please let me know."

Work was not showing up in Los Angeles and neither were places to stay, not even rooms to rent, despite the fact that she was looking hard. It didn't feel like the answer was to stay because there was nothing coming in to sustain her current situation and she had no roots to keep her where she was—no children, no family in L.A., no fulfilling career or even a job that could provide for her financially.

One day, Connie had the impulse to check out the Yoga Works Facebook page. Yoga Works is a California-based yoga studio and Connie is a graduate of their teacher training program. She occasionally used their Facebook page for inspiration and to be kept abreast of what was happening in the yoga community, but had not visited the page for many, many months. On the day she visited, the top post was from a teacher she knew of but had not met. He wrote about international teaching and she connected deeply with his words.

Because she didn't know him personally, reaching out to him felt intimidating, but she faced her fear and did anyway. He had a few ideas and suggestions for her, but the last bit of information he shared really caught her attention. He said he knew of a couple with a bed and breakfast in Costa Rica who might be looking for a yoga instructor. But it would include a job as—ta da! —a bartender during the off hours, so she'd need to know how to do that, too. Did she want him to pass on her name? Connie felt an immediate connection and a "yes!" to the possibility. She said yes to the teacher passing her name on, but then tried to take a stance of asking, trusting, and letting it go. She went about trusting that the answer would reveal itself. She let go of fear.

In the meantime, as part of her letting-go process and to earn some money, she sold the things she'd had to put in storage when she was staying at different places in L.A. with friends or housesitting for people. She had to sell everything for a tiny fraction of what it was worth or, as she described it, "for pennies." However, doing so released energetic attachment and created a huge opening. It was a symbolic statement that she was not rooted in, nor to, L.A.

Fear would have had her hang onto her possessions—it was everything she owned, and she would need those things when she got back on her feet. But she also knew she needed to let go.

The next day, she heard about the opening in Costa Rica.

An email came that the couple in Costa Rica wanted to hire her! They would provide room and board and pay her to teach. She'd be living at the beach, teaching yoga during the day, and working at the cantina at night!

It was brave to go off to Costa Rica for a year, not knowing a soul there or quite what to expect. All she knew was that she asked for this and it arrived, so she said yes to it. She used the Love Versus Fear tool in Costa Rica as well, when adventures showed up like diving in the ocean or going for long solo hikes in secluded areas. She relied heavily on this tool and it always served her well. She is now back and says that her trip was the highlight of her life so far and that she has grown in ways previously unimaginable to her.

And now she is ready for her next adventure.

* * *

Love makes your soul crawl out from its hiding place.

—Zora Neale Hurston

Now, IN THIS MOMENT, REMEMBER a time when you were deeply in love. This can be with another person or with a pet. It might be a time you were just falling in love or a time when you dropped into a deeper love and love took a plunge to a new level. Plug back into that feeling for a moment. What emotions flooded your brain and body? Maybe excitement and joy? Exuberance? Hope? *Glee?!* Wonderment?

And how did your heart feel? Maybe fuller? Did you feel more alive and happier? Did days seem a little brighter and easier to get through, perhaps? That's love strutting her stuff. When your soul is enlightened with love and you're looking out at the world through the eyes of love, you're kind of buzzing. Let's call that buzzing your "vibration" or "frequency."

When you are in a place of love, you operate at a higher frequency. When you are in fear, you are constricted and vibrate at a lower frequency. If you live your life in fear, not just situationally but always, your life is not as fun or interesting. You are far from buzzing. You are the opposite. In this state, you repel positive experiences and may be a magnet for the negative. You will see negativity all around you, and since that is where you're focused, you will draw in more of it.

Basically, love kicks fear's ass.

In a loving way, of course!

Think of the woman mentioned in the beginning of the book who wanted to attract dating, relationships, and eventually marriage into her life but wasn't even going on a single date. She deeply desired a partner for life. But unconsciously, she thought marriage would trap her. She felt stifled in her first marriage and thought that was what marriage looked and felt like. She was clear that she did not want *that* again.

Fear was getting in the way of her receiving the love she wanted and so richly deserved. When she realized that fear had shown up to protect her from further disappointment and had her unconsciously repelling men, she thanked fear for showing up and then showed it to the door. Soon thereafter she had several amazing, eligible, doting men in her life to date because love had room to step in.

This is not to say that fear is always unwarranted, or that we shouldn't pay attention. If we get instinctively that we shouldn't walk down a particular street because something about it gives us the creeps, or we get a bad feeling about a person, we must trust that. Fear tries to protect us. Fear showing up can save our life. Fear can tell us it's time for fight or flight.

Sometimes that fear is a limiting belief based on a bad past experience or is our Shadow or worrying what others might think. And sometimes fear is your own honest intuition. Listen to your body and thoughts when fear speaks, and you will be able to tell the difference.

Love wants to know itself through you. Let her in.

* * *

REMEMBER THAT FEAR CAN SERVE a purpose, but love is the place we want to strive to come from, the majority of our lives. Love feels better, gives us better outcomes, and is a higher frequency.

If the terms "vibration" or "frequency" seem far out and too "woo-woo" for you, consider this: How many times have you gotten a sense of a person or situation from the energy? For example, you decided not to stay at a party that was getting too wild and out of hand. Or said about someone, "She has the best energy! I just love being around her!" Or, "I don't get a good feeling about that person. I don't trust him. He has negative juju." That was you plugging into energy.

Living in the frequency of love as much as possible means we are heart-centered in thought, word, and deed. It means we project the high frequency of love and light and it returns to us. This is the Law of Attraction. It's the Law of Reciprocity. More good flows to you, but not because you are forcing it or "doing" anything. You are just being. Your goodness begets goodness. Being more heart-centered, open, and loving, you are more in the flow of life. You respond more enthusiastically to life and life responds more enthusiastically to you.

* * *

THE FOLLOWING SUGGESTIONS MIGHT SOUND simplistic, but the benefits of doing them consistently will have a long-term effect. First of all, focusing your attention on places that are loving versus places that make you feel afraid will affect how you feel and how you view the world. You might consider switching off or limiting television news, which is pretty much a steady stream of all that is negative in sound-bite form, and replacing it with listening to news from a source that gives you longer, more detailed, and informed versions of what is currently happening. National Public Radio is an intelligent source for that. And NPR isn't just news, but also engaging stories, in-depth interviews, and reporting—information and not just constant headlines. Or you could get your news from a newspaper you like. That way, you can decide not to read something if to do so would create anxiety and fear in you, whereas you can't unsee something from television. Likewise, social media can be filled with depressing posts and anxiety-provoking rants that drain our energy. Consider giving yourself a social media vacation.

The same is true of the movies you see or shows you watch on television. If you find that you continually replay scary scenes from movies in your mind and are bothered by them, or if watching violence on TV before bedtime makes it difficult to fall asleep, consider putting yourself on a viewing diet. If this is the case for you, a good rule of thumb is, if it would be traumatizing to see something in person, don't put yourself in a position to see it on a screen. Don't invite such images into your psyche (and living room!). A constant diet of them can desensitize us to violence, create a feeling of disconnection from others and have us on a kind of high alert.

It's easier to come from love when you turn your attention toward positivity and inviting in things, people, and situations that make you happy while removing habits that lower your vibration, like eating poorly, hanging out with negative people, listening to or engaging in gossip, and watching violence in movies and on television.

Some things that makes us connect more deeply to love and raise our energy and vibration, thus shifting us to a higher frequency, are being with other positive people, surrounding ourselves with beauty such as art and nature, going to the beach and soaking in the warm sun, and listening to the rhythmic beat of the tide. Hiking, especially going to the top of a hill or mountain and getting a higher point of view, raises our energy and vibration too. Certain music is said to raise it, particularly music recorded with a frequency at 528 Hertz, which has been shown to resonate with the energy of love, peace, and health. John Lennon recorded his famous song "Imagine," an enduring hymn to peace and promise, at this frequency. Award-winning humanitarian author Dr. Leonard Horowitz calls 528 Hz "God's 'C' Note."

OTHER WAYS WE RAISE OUR LOVE QUOTIENT

Avoid gossip.

Practice acts of kindness and giving to others without expecting anything in return.

Be grateful and focus on all you have and are thankful for versus focusing on what you do not have.

Eat healthfully, avoiding highly processed and chemical-laden foods and eat organic, fresh food as much as possible. Notice how certain foods make you feel.

Travel to places that make you feel peaceful or are known for having good energy themselves, like Sedona, Hawaii, or the mountains, to raise your energy and vibration.

Meditation, too, can raise our frequency and make us feel calm by settling down our nervous system and quieting the chatter (known as "monkey mind" because our inner chatter swings from thing to thing).

Yoga is helpful for this as well.

All of these are things you can do to fall more deeply into a state of love, thereby helping you come from love more than fear.

* * *

HOW ELSE CAN YOU COME from love in each moment, other than by checking in with your body and listening to the words you use around the choice you are about to make? One thing I do in my own life and teach my clients to do is take a breath, close your eyes, and ask the question, "What would love have me do here?" And then just settle in and hear or feel what comes to you. Be still and see what answer comes up to the surface for you.

* * *

Love takes off masks that we fear we cannot live
without and know we cannot live within.

—James Baldwin

NO DISCUSSION ON LEARNING TO come from love and being loving would be complete without mentioning the importance of self-love.

It's where everything begins. *You can't love others unless you love yourself first.*

LOVE VERSUS FEAR EXERCISES

1. How can you benefit today from observing, not judging, where you are in your ability to come from love instead of fear? Can you remember some recent examples? Journal about them.

2. I claimed earlier that love operates on a higher frequency than fear. An experiential way to know this is to try this simple exercise. Think of a difficult person with whom you are having a problem or struggle right now. Close your eyes and really see and feel them. How do you feel when you think of them?

   Now think about what you love about them. It may be hard at first, but take your time. Really think about the things you love about this person. Send them love as well. Has your feeling shifted now that you have thought of things you love about them? This is an example of raising your vibration or frequency to a level of love. It's as if you were listening to the radio and it was not quite on the station, so you turned the dial and found the right frequency.

   Sounds a lot better, doesn't it?

3. Our energy is a magnet. It attracts experiences into our lives that match our energetic field. What is happening outside in your world is a reflection of what is going on inside. If you don't like the experiences you are having, ask yourself what energy you are putting out. Take some personal responsibility

for the fact that the life you are living may be a reflection of you and, if you want different outcomes, you'll have to provide different inputs. Become mindful of (that is, observe) the energy you are putting out. Journal about what you discover.

4. Connecting to or expanding your *physical* heart can create an expansion of your heart center (or "heart chakra"). The heart chakra, your fourth chakra, is located at the center of your physical heart. It also is midpoint between the lower three chakras, which are related to our grounded, earthly bodies (safety, relationship to self and others, and relationship to sex), and the upper three chakras, which are related to voice, enlightenment, and connecting to the Divine. Here are some enjoyable ways to do that.

   a. You can do some simple yoga poses to balance and open the heart chakra. These poses stretch tense muscles in your chest and open your heart space. You do not have to be a seasoned yoga practitioner to do (in no particular order) the sphinx pose, camel pose, cat pose, fish pose, and chest fly. Instructions for doing these poses can be found online, in books, or at a yoga studio.

   b. Hug heart-to-heart! We tend to hug with our hearts on opposite sides. It may take some fun practice at first and a little bobbing of the head from side to side, but try getting into the habit of hugging so that both of your hearts align when you hug someone (in other words, your left and their left).

   c. Exercise the pectoral area by doing activities such as swimming or pushups.

d. Express yourself. Using your voice and expressing your feelings and thoughts opens your heart, whereas suppression creates constriction.

e. Have a one-on-one with fear. When fear shows up, treat it as you would a little child. Maybe even picture yourself as the cute and innocent little boy or girl you were. Let fear sit near you and express itself. Tell that vulnerable child that you are there, that you are listening. Don't cut fear off or dismiss it as nonsense. Ask it what it wants you to know. Let the child go into what is coming up for her. Maybe she will tell you that the current, scary-feeling situation is reminiscent of something that happened in the past and was very hurtful or dreadful and she's is afraid it's going to happen again. Listen to her. Tell her that her feelings make sense and that you hear her. Tell her you appreciate her showing up and trying to protect you from being blindsided. Then tell her that your adult self has "got this." Tell her you will be okay. And then release fear.

When we face fear, it goes away. Not because we pushed it underground and pretended it wasn't there. That never works. That makes it fester and show up in uncomfortable ways. Facing feelings, any feelings, tends to them.

Keep in mind, *the suffering that our fear causes us becomes greater than our fear of facing it.*

CHAPTER 8
TOOL 6: THE MAGIC OF SYNCHRONICITY

I do believe in an everyday sort of magic—the
inexplicable connectedness we sometimes experience
with places, people, works of art and the like;
the eerie appropriateness of moments of synchronicity;
the whispered voice, the hidden presence,
when we think we're alone.

—Charles de Lint

SYNCHRONICITIES ARE MEANINGFUL COINCIDENCES AND signs
that we are on track. They're placed here as the sixth tool because
once you have opened yourself to ask and receive from the Universe,
it's nice to get road signs that you are on the right track.

Without them, we might be tempted to pull ourselves back to
our old way of being when wounds like "I don't get to have" pop
up. Synchronicity calls to us and says, "You're on the right track!"
Or, "You are not alone!" And once you are aware of synchronicity,
you can open yourself to even more messages if you know how.

This is my favorite tool of all because it's the most *fun*! It's as
if you and the Universe are dancing together! A definition is in

order because people often get "synchronicity," "serendipity," and "coincidence" confused.

Going from the least to most significant, for purposes of clarification, let's start with coincidence. A coincidence is a meaningless but fun occurrence of fact. For example, I find out your mother's name is Beth Green and she grew up in Wichita. "That's funny!" I say. "*My* mom's name was Beth Green and *she* grew up in Wichita too!" The coincidence is uncanny, but there's really no relevance to it. You'd call it "chance" or "happenstance."

Serendipity, on the other hand, is a lucky coincidence wherein something positive comes from chance. For example, that guy you meant to call to ask for advice, but hadn't found time to connect with yet, was at the obscure little market at the same time you were and you were able to finally get your question answered. This is an example of a "lucky" coincidence. There is a happy bit of luck to things going the way they did. You'd call it "fortuitous."

Here is an example of serendipity that happened in my own life, a slice of lucky coincidence. One morning I went for a run. I took the same route I had taken nearly every day for more than five years: one and a half miles straight south from my house to a traffic signal, and then back north the same way I came. On this particular morning, I decided to turn left and run down the sidewalk instead of turning around to go back home when I got to the signal. I had never done that before and couldn't explain why I wanted to this time, but I felt a pull I could not ignore. I listened and went.

Two steps in that direction and I saw a wallet on the ground. I opened it up and found the owner's name and phone number and ran home with it so I could give the owner a call and let her know I had found it. When I called the wallet's owner and set up a time to come by to give it to her, she told me that she knew she lost it and put out a prayer that "someone honest" would find it and return it to her. Her intention for it to be found and my instinct to turn left at the signal somehow "met" in the middle and the wallet was returned. All of it was very fortuitous, and it feels good when things like this happen, but it's *not* synchronicity.

Synchronicity is distinct because of its almost magical element; the likelihood of things going the way they did are just too far out, as if they were aligned.

Synchronicity does not have a cause and effect, so is therefore acausal. But it does feel meaningfully connected.

One example of it might be that you're lying in bed in the morning and suddenly begin to think about your best friend from high school, whom you haven't thought of in years. You had good times together and have always had warm feelings for this person, and you start wondering what happened to her and thinking it would be nice to be in touch to find out. But you have no idea how to reach her. Suddenly, your phone rings, you pick it up, and it's that friend. Your thinking about that person didn't cause her to call. There is a kind of fusion between the inner and outer world when synchronicity happens. You will think of someone, or have a dream or vision from the inner world, and then something will show up in the outer world that is a kind of "match" to that inner thought or vision.

Sometimes people have a dream about something that will show up later in their waking state, like hearing from a person we just dreamed of or getting an answer to something in a dream that we were struggling with in waking life. When synchronicities happen, it feels a bit mind-blowing!

Carl Jung, Swiss psychiatrist and founder of analytical psychology, studied the phenomenon of synchronicity for more than twenty years before he published his thoughts on it. He felt it was one of his most profound discoveries because he understood the impact that becoming aware of synchronicities can have on our lives. He grasped that knowing how to interpret the synchronicities in our life can guide us when we are stuck, help us solve issues, or provide us comfort when we are struggling.

The following story from his own work will show how right he was.

He brings up an experience a patient of his had with a scarab, an exotic and beautiful blue-green beetle. He writes about it in his book *Synchronicity* (1952).

My example concerns a young woman patient who, in spite of efforts made on both sides, proved to be psychologically inaccessible. The difficulty lay in the fact that she always knew better about everything.

After several fruitless attempts to sweeten her rationalism with a somewhat more human understanding, I had to confine myself to the hope that something unexpected and irrational would turn up, something that would burst the intellectual defense into which she had sealed herself. Well, I was sitting opposite her one day, with my back to the window, listening to her flow of rhetoric. She had an impressive dream the night before, in which someone had given her a golden scarab—a costly piece of jewelry. While she was still telling me this dream, I heard something behind me gently tapping on the window. I turned around and saw that it was a fairly large flying insect that was knocking against the window-pane from outside in the obvious effort to get into the dark room. This seemed to me very strange. I opened the window immediately and caught the insect in the air as it flew in. It was a scarab beetle. I handed the beetle to my patient with the words, "Here is your scarab."

This experience punctured the desired hole in her rationalism and broke the ice of her intellectual resistance. The treatment could now be continued with satisfactory results.

Jung quite literally handed his patient the link between her waking and dreaming states. She realized her dream from the previous night was reenacted when she was wide awake in Jung's office. Writings about this experience say that the shock of realizing this and understanding its meaning "cracked her defensive shell wide open" and that a fundamental shift happened that transformed her and made her more open and receptive.

The same can be said for people in deep grief who may be closed off until they see signs, which they believe to be messages from their departed loved ones on the other side, that cannot be mere coincidences.

After my parents passed away eleven weeks apart and just shy of their sixty-year anniversary, we had a large joint memorial service and then a private one for just my two sisters and me, our husbands, another couple, and the two owners of the boat in which we sailed around the San Francisco Bay. On the boat, we had a small, private ceremony and then scattered their ashes together in the Bay. When the last poem was read, the last prayer was said, and we were finished releasing ashes to the water, suddenly two dolphins that none of us had seen even once before during the trip swam off side by side from right next to the boat and away from us.

"And there they go," someone said.

Dolphins, in Greek mythology and animal symbolism, are said to carry the spirits of the dead over to the other side. And so interesting that there were *two*, side by side, leaving our boat. None of us saw them before that one brief moment in time just after the service and none of the ten of us saw them again that day.

When synchronicity happens, it can be so amazing and unbelievable that it stops us in our tracks, sometimes literally. It arrests our attention, and when we focus on it, we see that it has something important to tell us.

About a year after my mother passed away, I went for a run. Running was something she and my father did together, so I always feel especially connected to them when I hit the pavement. On this particular run, I started to think of her as I often do, but this time I started crying because I wanted to be in touch with her. My emotions were running high and I had some unfinished things I wanted to "talk" to her about.

After a few minutes of a conversation with her in my head, I wondered if she could even hear me. I felt not only sad, but incomplete. I asked if I could please have a sign that she was present, and then added through tears, "A heart-shaped rock would be nice."

Then I ran a few steps, and lo and behold, on the sidewalk in front of me was a heart-shaped rock! Not an "I-can-make-that-be-a-heart-if-I really-try" rock. A legit and clearly heart-shaped rock. I smiled, picked it up, and thanked her, laughing through my tears. In two more steps, there was another one. Then another. Then another. Four of them. Then I found a paper heart! Then one more heart-shaped rock! Six in all, pretty equally spaced, and in a straight line.

I carried the rock hearts home in my hand and her love in my heart.

It made me laugh. I had no doubt they were from her. The manner in which she did it was so *her*. It would be just like her to leave not just one sign, but a bunch to be sure I got the message. It also made me think of how she would go all out on Valentine's Day for us, even when my sisters and I were older. She would make hearts from construction paper, add doilies, and write sweet messages of love on them. Finding all the hearts in a row had a similar feel to those Valentine's Day homemade cards. To test the synchronicity of that experience since, I've often looked for heart-shaped rocks on that same sidewalk. It's the same path I run all the time, but I have never seen any since that day.

* * *

MELISSA, A MEMBER OF ONE of the Abundance Circles, lost her grandfather, Leo. She and her mother drove to the nursing home where he had been living to clean out his vacated room. On the way, they spoke about him and said it would be nice to get a sign from him. At that very moment, an old, beat-up white truck passed them. The side of the truck read, "Leo's Moving Company." They both noticed it, laughed, and felt reassured that it was the sign they had asked for.

* * *

A FEW YEARS AGO, I was doing grief work with a little girl. Her father was a well-known pop singer who had died very suddenly in an accident, leaving behind his wife, the daughter I was seeing, and two other small children, including an infant. I heard this story of synchronicity from the little girl's mother.

One night, when it was late and rainy, the infant got a high fever and needed to be rushed to the hospital. The other two children would need to be awakened and taken along since there was no one else home to stay with them. The mother felt anxious and scared. She wished her husband were there to go through it with her. Did the baby really need to go to the hospital then, or would he be okay staying at home through the night, with her vigilant care, and then going in the morning? She hated waking the other two and taking all of them out into the night. She also didn't want to frighten them with her worry or traumatize them by taking them from their beds and off to a strange place. If only she could stay home with the two older children while her husband took the baby to the hospital, or vice versa. Or what if something was terribly wrong and the baby died? All these thoughts and so much panic rang through her mind.

She woke her older children and got them, groggily, into the car. She fastened her infant into the car seat, driving carefully in the rain to the hospital, the water falling from the sky matching the tears falling down her face.

She missed her husband so much and longed for his input, company, and shoulder to lean on. This was a severe marker that she was really on her own now. She spoke to him in her mind all the way to the hospital, asking for a sign and for reassurance. Was the baby going to be okay? Was *she* going to be okay? Could he hear her? Was he "there"?

She got to the hospital and got the three children out of the car while asking her husband for some kind of a sign that it would be all right.

When she stepped into the bright lights of the lobby, she was struck by the music on the hospital sound system.

It was one of her late husband's songs.

Right then, she knew he had heard her and that everything was going to be all right, and it did in fact turn out all right for everyone. The infant was fine and, as it turned out, the older children found the late-night ride in the rain to be an adventure!

* * *

IN THE COURSE OF WRITING this book, I held live Abundance Circle gatherings based on these same tools (and I still do). One evening, without planning on it, a majority of the participants decided to give gifts to the others in the group, already a kind of synchronicity because that had never happened before. This night was not particularly different from the others. It wasn't anyone's birthday nor the last gathering, yet the majority of the members brought everyone else a present that night. So that by itself was very special and fun (as synchronicity always is).

But one thing in particular made it even more so.

One of the members had brought everyone beautiful gold bracelets with different inspiring sayings imprinted on them. They were wrapped and in a paper bag she held up as she walked in front of each of us. We each reached in and pulled out a bracelet without looking inside the bag. Without exception, the bracelet each person pulled out was absolutely meaningful for them.

One woman chose "Love." *That very morning* she had said to her husband, "I want to get a bracelet that says 'love' on it to remind myself to always come from love!" Another woman who has had two close brushes with death and lives by the credo, "live in the moment" chose a bracelet that said that very thing. And I, the leader of the Abundance Circles, pulled one that said, "Dream, Believe, Achieve," which is literally the motto of Abundance Circles.

It is always exciting when synchronicities happen to Abundance Circle participants while they are enrolled in a group, especially if synchronicity plays a part in conspiring to bring in the desired thing they spoke of in meeting number one. This happens often and in surprising, enchanting ways. Sometimes it happens even if people think the thing they desire is too remote for them to receive.

Two sweet examples:

Carolina is the woman mentioned earlier in the book whose deep desire was to go to Hawaii to visit her grandchildren. But she and her husband were facing bankruptcy, with their home in foreclosure, and she could not foresee such a trip happening in the near future.

Carolina is a young, vivacious California grandmother who was extremely involved with her grandchildren and saw them several times a week. When her daughter and grandchildren moved to Hawaii, Carolina was heartsick. She joined an Abundance Circle shortly after that and the intention she set was to somehow earn and save enough money to travel to Hawaii and visit them. However, despite deeply wanting this and wishing it could be true, she would tear up in the Circles and say that even if enough extra money were to miraculously come along, it would need to go toward the debt she and her husband were in and saving their home from foreclosure.

"It would be irresponsible to take a trip to Hawaii when we owe so much." The thought of losing their beloved home was harrowing; it made her cry to even think about it. And not seeing her grandchildren for who knew how long did the same. Her Abundance Circle group was supportive and continued to hold Carolina's vision with her. However, on paper, it looked quite dire.

And yet! About a month after the Circle ended, Carolina wrote a group email to her Abundance Circle. Out of the blue, her husband had been offered a job at the University of Hawaii in Honolulu, the very city where her grandchildren lived! They were told they could move in just a few months. They rented out their house, which provided more income—and allowed them to keep it! —and her husband had a nicely salaried position waiting for him on top of it!

Carolina not only sees her grandchildren again on a regular basis, but fulfilled a lifetime goal of going to college and getting her degree. She did this with nearly all the tuition paid for as an employee's spouse benefit. The Universe provided even more than she asked for.

To add to the synchronicity, when the two-year contract at the University ended, her husband was offered another job in Honolulu, this time at an Army Medical Hospital—the one that had saved his father's life decades before. His father had fought in the Korean War and was in a machine-gun nest when a grenade was thrown into it, seriously wounding him and killing all of his comrades. He would later receive a Purple Heart for his injuries that day. He was flown to the nearest hospital, where his life was saved: the hospital where Carolina's husband now works.

Carolina later wrote of this time, "I look back at that time in amazement! We rented out our home and packed the whole place up for the move in two months! Everything fell into place perfectly and that was no coincidence! I'll never forget how life has literally changed thanks to you putting together that miraculous circle!"

* * *

HERE IS YET ANOTHER SWEET example of synchronicity. Melinda was someone who wanted to call in a new partner and job opportunity and told her Abundance Circle group this on her first night. She had been single for more than a year after getting out of a very long relationship. That relationship taught her both what she did and did not want in a future relationship.

After speaking her desire to meet someone out loud in the group, she decided to sign up for online dating. This is an example of the work piece in Deep Desire + Work. She had been reluctant to do this again—she had done it before but found it a somewhat unpleasant experience—but felt it was the most realistic way to meet someone, so took the leap. She wrote out the qualities she desired in a partner, but stayed unattached to how he would show up.

Her third online date was with a guy named Tim. During their first couple of dates, they discovered that they had many things in common, including that these two California transplants shared some personal background. His parents now live in the tiny town of Calabash, North Carolina, a town Melinda visited every summer as a little girl with her grandmother and cousins. Her relatives lived in Myrtle Beach, South Carolina, but together they made the thirty-minute drive to that little spot. She has a photograph of herself sitting on the porch of a small ice cream parlor in the town Tim's parents live in now, and Tim knows that shop well. They learned of this while on their dates in Los Angeles. They also learned that they had lived *less than a mile* apart in Los Angeles for fifteen years! Before they met, however, Melinda moved from Los Angeles to Santa Monica, about forty-five minutes away, to be closer to the beach. They literally kept missing each other.

During this period, when Melinda wrote in her journal, she kept picking up something about New York and North Carolina, but didn't know what it meant.

Then one day in an Abundance Circle, after her group had met for several sessions, she told them that she thought she had met The One. By date number three with Tim, they'd both discovered how much they had in common and that they enjoyed doing a lot of the same things. They felt immediately comfortable together. He kept saying that something about her seemed familiar, like he had met her before, but that also seemed unlikely.

About a month into their relationship, Tim was at Melinda's home by the ocean, looking at her acting and modeling portfolio and watching a reel of some of her films and commercials, and said he also wanted to see her print ads. Tim was—and still is—very supportive of her work and wanted to see everything. Melinda went to get the envelope they were in and scattered the contents on the floor where they could look at everything together. In that pile was a book. A vampire romance novel, of all things! The cover was a photograph of two vampires, one male and one female, embracing in profile.

Tim picked up the book and stared. The room grew quiet. Melinda asked what he was thinking. He said, "I know this book. Over a decade ago I was in a bookstore with some friends and the cover of this novel caught my attention. My sister used to love these kinds of books. I bought a copy and inscribed it and sent it to my sister. I could not take my eyes off this book." After that bookstore visit, Tim went back to the shop several times just to look at the cover of that book.

Tim said to Melinda, "My friends were with me in the bookstore one day, and came over to me and asked what I was staring at. I could not stop staring at the woman on the cover. I said to them, 'This is the woman I want. She's perfect. This is the woman I want to be with.'"

Even as he said all this to her, his expression was one of shock. He was just stunned that she would have the book he had connected with so deeply, especially because the book was so obscure. It was so weird to see it again after all this time. Why would Melinda have a vampire romance novel in her home, of all things?

She said, "Tim! That's *me* on the cover."

They are still together, and she says of that time, "Everything makes sense to me now, and I learned a valuable lesson about patience and timing. Timing is everything. We have to trust that everything is on the way. We have to know and really believe what we want is on its way and when it is the right time, it will show up."

So, the North Carolina and New York piece that kept inexplicably showing up for Melinda? Melinda is from North Carolina and Tim's parents live there, and Tim is from New York. He went to film school there. The man she was going to be with had a strong connection to two states and she somehow picked up on those places without knowing why. She just "noted" it. She observed the thought a few times but wasn't attached to it. However, it *was* meaningful.

Pay attention to the things that keep showing up, even when you don't understand their meaning.

Melinda has let go of her acting and modeling and taken a leap to do a job she created that combines her love of wine and dogs. It's wildly creative and successful, so the job opportunity piece that she originally longed for in session one of her Abundance Circle happened too.

"I *love* that I brought Tim into my life during the Abundance Circle and that things lined up so magically!"

Tim is pretty happy about that too!

* * *

THE SIGNS OF SYNCHRONICITY CAN come in countless ways. Our only job is to be open to them. They can arrive as songs that come on with a perfect message at the right moment, in recurring numbers such as 11:11, or on literal signs like license plates, billboards, or the side of a truck.

Have you ever ordered a cappuccino at a café and found that when the waiter brought it to you, he had put a little biscotti or piece of dark chocolate on the saucer along with your espresso? If so, how did that make you feel? When it happens to me, it feels special. I feel happy and pleasantly surprised and I feel a warmer connection to the waiter.

That's how it is when synchronicity happens: we feel supported, cared about, and pleasantly surprised. The Universe (the waiter) says to us, in essence, "I'll give you what you ordered and more." A kind of "I'll see you and raise you one!" One time I was washing dishes in my kitchen and decided I'd like to have some "company" as I did. I thought, "Hmmm. Do I want to put on a Jackson Browne CD or listen to NPR on the kitchen radio?"

I decided I wanted to listen to NPR. I turned on the kitchen radio and what was playing in that very moment was "You Love the Thunder" by Jackson Browne! And I smiled and let the fun of that moment sink in and thought to myself, *"You just got both!"*

So delicious when that happens.

These were small and common occurrences, but the power of this tool is in appreciating these events. Don't let them go by without appreciating their wonder.

SYNCHRONICITY EXERCISES

1. Observe how synchronicity did or did not show up for you this week. Journal about your experiences, or even what the subject of synchronicity brings up for you, to deepen your connection to it.

2. One of the most effective ways to bring in synchronicity is just being open to receiving the wisdom and grateful when it appears. In other words, ask for synchronicity by setting a clear intention for it to happen, like asking my mother in spirit for the heart-shaped rocks. Then, when it happens, be present and aware of it. See if there is a particular meaning in the *way* your synchronicity keeps showing up. For example, if you keep seeing dragonflies, butterflies, or a specific number, or a rare occurrence crosses your path, like a bird or animal

coming close to you, look up the symbolism of these things in addition to being aware of them continually showing up.

3. Express gratitude for it happening.

CHAPTER 9
TOOL 7: GRACE AND GRATITUDE

Acknowledging the good that you already have in your
life is the foundation for all abundance.

—Eckhart Tolle, *A New Earth*

THE FINAL TOOL IS, LIKE the first one, a double one: grace and
gratitude.

But what is grace exactly? It has kind of an old-fashioned feel
and isn't a term we hear very often anymore. Might even sound a
little sentimental, quaint, or naïve. Maybe the only time you heard
it used in this context was a time you heard your grandma or great-
grandma sing "Amazing Grace." But what is it about grace that is
so amazing?

Grace is that thing that shows up when life gets hard or you don't
see a way out and rescues your butt from a seemingly inescapable
situation.

"Of all the things that exist, we breathe and wake and turn it into
song," Mark Nepo reminds us. That is what grace looks like. Taking
all that is and turning it into song. Grace is the gift. Gratitude is
being reverently appreciative of that gift.

When my twin and I were about seven years old, we made up
something while we were in the ocean on summer vacation and said

it every time we were in thereafter. We would go out to where the waves were coming in to bodysurf, play with the waves and allow them to take our skinny little one-piece bathing-suited bodies from rolling waves to shore and back to waves again.

Most of the time, you can work out a kind of rhythm and dance with the waves where you're getting along pretty well and it feels more like being carried to shore than as if two tons just landed on your head and you can say so long to the thought of ever seeing your parents or pet rabbit again. Sometimes, though, the ocean crashes down on you so hard and you're under so long you think, "This is it! So long, World!"

There is a spot, when you're bodysurfing where the wave starts to swell but you are too far away from it to ride it in, yet too far away from the shore to run slo-mo in water back to it and just *skip* that wave. So you're stuck. Can't get to it; can't get away from it. My twin and I used to call this the "sticky spot." We'd shout, "Oh! Oh! We are in a sticky spot!" We knew that the only thing you could do was dive toward the wave and let it pass over you while you held your ground (and breath) as best you could.

Well, grace is what saves you in times when your life is in a "sticky spot." It shows up when you least expect it and rescues you. It's like your get-out-of-jail-free card. It's you finding a way out of no way.

You can think of grace as being the first cousin to mercy. But the way I see the two, mercy shows up in life and says, "Here you are. I feel sorry for you. Take this."

Grace, on the other hand, shows up and says, "Here you are. I feel love for you. Take this." It shows up because we are loved in a benevolent Universe and needed the assistance.

GRATITUDE

As we receive what we have desired or needed, it is right and good to give thanks. When someone makes or buys you a gift, wraps it, and then gives it to you, thanking that person completes the cycle.

Likewise, thanking the Universe for your gifts does the same. Imagine you give a friend a present and she takes it without acknowledging you at all. No smile, no saying she can use it or that she appreciates it, and definitely no thank-you note. She rips the paper and ribbon off and just looks at it, unmoved. This wouldn't feel very good. But when you give a gift to a loved one and they give a huge smile, say that they love it and it's just what they always wanted, that they have the perfect place for it, that they will think of you whenever they see it and they jump up and down and hug you—doesn't it make you happy to see them happy? Doesn't it make you more inclined to give to them? Your vibration matches their vibration!

Similarly, the Universe may be a benevolent place and certainly it provides for us lovingly and abundantly. The more grateful we are for the gifts it provides, the more it gives. Perhaps the grateful person is an optimistic person and therefore sees the gifts in life. The negative person may not even see the big, lovely gift-wrapped present the Universe places in their lap, let alone give thanks for it. But the law of reciprocity says in order to receive, we have to also give. A simple example of this is, when given a gift, give a "thank you." If you want money, give money. If you want joy, give joy. If you want love, give love.

You get the picture. Give what you want more of. It is the same with the Universe's dance with us. When you receive (Tool 2!) from the Universe in any form, take a moment to pause, be in a state of gratitude, and *give* thanks. Receive with grace. This applies to both the tangible and the unseen. Answers to your soul's requests, things that you need showing up at exactly the right time, feeling connected or at peace—all of these deserve a moment of quiet reflection and thanksgiving.

Receiving gifts with grace means we receive fully and in an uncomplicated way. We don't deny the giver or reject the gift. I am using the word *receiving* to denote graciousness. Have you ever complimented someone on their hair or clothes and they said, "This old thing?!" or something similarly dismissive? That is akin to reaching toward someone with a gift in your hands and have them slap it out of your hands. That is the opposite of grace.

Grace has us humbly accepting the gift while also feeling deserving. It is letting the gift "in." Imagine how Audrey Hepburn or Grace Kelly would receive a gift. Or Idris Elba or Sidney Poitier. That is how I imagine receiving gifts from the Universe with grace. Jacqueline Kennedy was famous for her beautiful, thoughtful, and personalized thank-you notes. Writing them was something she was taught to do as a little girl and carried into her adulthood. She made them personal by stating what made the gift so special and memorable to her. She was specific about the gift received and spelled it out.

Dear Richard—

What an eye you have and how lucky am I to be its beneficiary. You can't know how much I love the ancient Florentine book box. It is an object I will love forever.
I thank you so very much and send you all my happiest wishes for the New Year.

Jacqueline

Her thank-you notes were always written within twenty-four hours of receiving a gift. And she didn't just write them for physical gifts. Dignitaries who attended the dinners hosted by the Kennedys and those who hosted them, interior and fashion designers, children who wrote her letters—they all received notes of thanks. So did her personal maid, the White House photographer, and her chef that made the mango ice cream she loved. All received handwritten thank-you notes from this admirable woman when she was the First Lady of the United States.

The most unfathomable and awe-inspiring act of class and grace she displayed with her notes came after her husband was shot as she sat next to him in an open convertible in Dallas in 1963. Some 1.5 million mourners sent their condolences to the mourning First Lady. She responded to many of them.

* * *

WHAT IS YOUR PERSONAL, HANDWRITTEN thank you to the Universe? How do you elegantly and graciously thank the Universe for the gifts you are given? A gift can be a job showing up that you asked for, or the right person showing up to help in just the way you need it at just the right time. It can be when you get the feeling out of the blue that you should pick up a particular book or go to a yoga class or a movie and that book, class, or movie has a message that is exactly what you need to hear. It can be when someone shows up with a thing you can hold in your hand and it, or the gesture, lifts your spirits just when you need it.

That means "gifts" are more than physical objects—they can be seen or unseen things in our lives. Either way, the more we say thank you for them and the more we receive them with grace, the more we receive. Then, the more we give back. And the more we receive. And so on. On and on it goes, this Law of Reciprocity. It's part of what we are doing here. Learning to dance with each other and with the Universe, learning to give and take.

Grace, the continual outpouring of favors and gifts from a loving Universe before we have even asked, is ours for the receiving, here for our benefit if we only have eyes to see it. There is already bountiful abundance around and within us. We have a storehouse of gifts, talents, and attributes inside us. How often do we remember to thank the Universe for our inherent gifts, the things we arrived with, like our warmth that attracts others, our artistic abilities, or our intellect? Start there.

Claire was a member of one of my Abundance Circle groups. She had stated that she wanted to attract a new place to live and employment. In short order, she manifested a place that seemed to be all she desired, down to having the treehouse feel she had imagined! The landlady also accepted her cat, something not everyone leasing spaces was willing to do, and it was close to work, not always a given in Los Angeles! She was able to do this when there were not a lot of places available and on the market.

That was her first manifesting success out of the Circle. Then she manifested a job in her field that seemed to be a good one and provided her with the finances she needed and an outlet for her massive creative capabilities. Although it was to be temporary, it was very close to what she had put out to the Universe that she needed. Her Abundance Circle cheered at her news!

It was perfect!

For a while.

After her round of the Abundance Circles ended, I got a call from her. She shared with me the following story.

She had been working at the job that came in during her time in the Abundance Circle for three months. But one afternoon without any warning she had been let go.

Of course she was shocked, devastated, and angry. She thought she would be there longer. She tried to discuss the dismissal with her boss but he had made up his mind. She tried to defend herself and ask questions, but he was adamant and his decision final. She left the room shakily and went down to her car. When she got in, she pulled out her phone. She wanted to make a call to a friend for support, but while it was in her hand, it rang! It was a colleague from the job she had before she got the temporary one while in the Abundance Circle. The colleague said that she had gotten a job offer from a well-known company that paid well and looked fantastic, but was not really in her skill set. She thought it would be perfect for Claire. She added, "But you need to call *now* to tell them you are interested. They haven't even announced this job and it's going to be filled soon because everyone wants to work at "X"! You'd be perfect for what they are looking for. It wasn't a fit for me, but it *is* for you! Call right now. Here's the number and the person to speak to!"

It should be noted that it is unheard of for this company to interview people they haven't reached out to themselves.

So Claire, still shaken from what had literally just happened, took some breaths and made the call. After her contact got some basic information about Claire's work background, she made an appointment for an interview for the very next day. Claire went to the interview and was excited by the things she heard about the position. It would combine all the things she really wanted in her career. It was at a company she had always wanted to work for. Jobs there are in demand and extremely hard to get. The job would combine several things she always wanted to do and was highly qualified for, and in fact the job was a new one in the field that utilized many of her skills. As she listened in the interview, she thought, "I didn't even know jobs like this existed." As it turns out, they hadn't until this one!

She aced the interview. She got the job! The interview was at 2:30 and she was at work the next morning at 9:00 a.m.!

She had the job one day after the interview thanks to a lead she got within minutes of being fired from the previous one. And the pay was great on top of it: more than she had gotten before and more than she had asked the Universe for when she described the kind of job she desired.

The temp job was just a placeholder, something to fill in her time while this new job was being created. Created for *her*, it would seem.

The temporary job was there when she needed it, after the first one ended but while the new one, the job of her dreams, was still being created. It did what it was supposed to do. It provided her with money when she needed it. Then, when that job did what it was meant to in her life and was no longer needed, a better one, the *right* one, came along.

One door closed. Another opened.

She called me to tell me she believed that using the tools from the Abundance Circle—and adding the phrase, "This or something better" which I teach people to do when sending out their requests—was behind her ability to call this in so quickly. This job had everything she'd said she was looking for in her first Abundance Circles group session, but also, truly, so much more. Including things she hadn't even dared ask for.

That is what grace looks like.

Ask. Believe. Receive.

Even

After
All this time
The Sun never says to the Earth,

"You owe me."

Look
What happens
With a love like that,
It lights the whole sky.

—Hafiz, fourteenth-century Persian poet

Living in grace and gratitude brings us joy, and joy is our birthright. What blocks our joy is being separated from love. Coming from a place of grace and gratitude as often as possible brings more joy and opens the door to love.

When I was in high school and college, I would sometimes write out the word "Joy!" with its exclamation point in large, beautiful script across whatever homework I was doing or on notes I was taking when the mood struck. I hadn't been taught to do it and wasn't doing it to "make" myself feel happy. I was just moved to do so, and it always felt so uplifting to my soul. I was, in essence, coming home to the joy that resides in my own heart and connecting to it. When we are in joy (*enjoy!*), grace and gratitude are nearby, and the other way around, too.

One way to stand in grace is to become mindful. Begin with where you are. Begin with a clear mind so your thoughts are kind and pure. Imagine a pure white light washing through your mind and holding positive, loving thoughts there. Where you might in the past have judged someone for behaving poorly or reacting to something differently than you would, show compassion instead. When your first reaction is to judge something, ask yourself instead, "What would compassion have me do here?"

And when things are rough in life, see where the gift or lesson is rather than judging or becoming cynical. Ask, "What is this here to teach me?" Life isn't good and bad. It's good and rough. The hard things we face and go through often come as our teachers and bring important lessons. When we seek the lesson and gift, even the rough stuff can be beneficial.

And the gift in the rough stuff is another way of saying, simply, "grace."

Now see that white light come down from your mind and behind your eyes so you see the good. See the good in yourself, in others, and in the world. Seek beauty in everything you look at.

Next, see it come down and settle behind your mouth so that your words are helpful, truthful, and kind. Eliminate gossip. Thoughts, sight, and words, all as kind and full of thanks as can be. *Gratitude is the road grace begins her journey on.*

Clear mind and clear thinking.

Clear eyes and clear seeing.

Clear mouth and clear speaking.

Grace is also learning to see life's circumstances without any judgment or labels, just an acceptance of what is, as often as possible.

An example of this is the ancient Taoist story of an old farmer and his horse. Its origin is unknown but is said to have been a favorite of Lao Tzu (born 601 BC). It goes like this:

Once upon a time there was an old poor farmer and his son who lived at the edge of a small village in China. The old farmer had worked his fields for many years. One day the farmer's horse ran away. Upon hearing the news, his neighbors came to pay their respect. "Such bad luck," they said sympathetically.

"Maybe," the farmer replied.

The next morning, the horse returned, bringing with it three other wild horses. "How wonderful," the neighbors exclaimed.

"Maybe," replied the old man.

The following day, his son got on the back of one of the untamed horses, was thrown off and broke his leg. The neighbors again came to offer their sympathy on his misfortune. "What terrible luck!" they told him.

"Maybe," answered the farmer.

The day after, the country was invaded, and military officials marched into the village to take away all the young men to serve in the army and fight in the war. Seeing that the son's leg was broken, the farmer's son was rejected. The neighbors congratulated the farmer on how well things had turned out.

"Maybe," said the farmer.

* * *

ANOTHER DEFINITION OF GRACE, BESIDES the one we used that has to do with a kind of unmerited favor or help is "simple elegance" and "refinement of movement." We say about a person, "She moved across the floor with effortless grace." How can you bring that kind of grace to your everyday life? Another definition of grace is to do honor to someone or dignify a situation by your presence, as in "She graced him with her presence" or "She bowed out of the sport she has graced for two decades." Imagine for a moment just a whiff of a fine perfume lingering in a room after someone has gone, leaving behind something beautiful, mysterious, and pleasant, and making the room a better place by having been there. That's what living in grace does.

It leaves the planet better for your having been there.

GRACE AND GRATITUDE EXERCISES

1. Observe, don't judge the places grace showed up for you today or this week. And observe, don't judge the places you came from gratitude. Just take quiet notice of it.

2. Instead of thinking in terms of things in life as "good" and "bad," consider thinking of them as "good" and "rough." When rough stuff happens, journal on "What is the lesson in this?" Try non-dominant handwriting for this. Write a question like, "What is my next step?" or "What is the lesson in this?" with your dominant hand. Then switch the pen to your other hand. In doing so, you access a different part of your brain by linking its left and right hemispheres. This taps you into both the conscious and unconscious reaches of your mind. Thoughts you hadn't already considered will come up through the exercise. My therapy clients have been using this technique for many years and have had very profound and often very surprising results.

CHAPTER 10
WRAPPING IT ALL UP IN A SHEER SILK RIBBON

You are now acquainted with seven tools you can carry like precious gems in your hands as you go through life, to use as you see fit and whenever your heart desires. Some of these tools may be new to you, or perhaps you knew of them but didn't pay a lot of attention to them. Some may be old acquaintances that have traveled alongside you much of your life. Whatever the case may be, from here on out, each of the seven tools can now be genuinely called upon as your constant companion to assist you in creating and manifesting the life you've always dreamed of having.

Knowing these tools now, which are you more aware of in your own life? And do you have a "favorite"?

You picked up this book because you desired to call in the thing that felt elusive to you, the one true thing your life felt incomplete without. Which tool was the most powerful in drawing that in for you?

What shifts have you seen in your life since implementing them?

As poet Mary Oliver's implores us in her poem "The Summer Day," "Tell me, what is it you plan to do with your one wild and precious life?" What will getting clear on your desires, and using these tools, create as you move forward? And, I wonder, what you plan to do with that precious, lit-up life?

YOUR MAGIC ELIXIR FOR STAYING ON TRACK

HERE IS YOUR MAGIC ELIXIR for the times you get stuck, go backwards, or sabotage yourself. When you feel overwhelmed and think something like, "Who am I to think I can have or do fill-in-the blank?", it's an opportunity to get outside of your thought and observe it. We have a tendency to want to stay comfortable with where we are. When we bump into a situation where we desire to self-sabotage, it's because two things are happening. One, we are getting out of the present moment. And two, we are afraid of growing and getting bigger. That's all! So the call to action is to observe that thought. Note it. Say, "Good to know that I still believe that." Because that thought tells you where you need to do some work. Don't judge the thought when you note it with "I should be past this now," or "I should know better." No, sir. Do not judge the thought or you will feel bad about both the stuck place and about occasionally having negative thoughts about where you are in your process. That's a double scoop of yucky. Stop "should-ing" on yourself. Seeing the old patterns that need revising is part of the growth and process. Not judging the thought helps keep you from sabotaging your inner work and yourself too. The desire to self-sabotage shows you where you need to do some tending.

Be an *observer* of the thought rather than a *believer*. If you observe an old wound, belief, or story coming up, you are in a position to course-correct to get the desired results.

When you see that you are close to self-sabotage, breathe deeply and see what tool might be handy to use as your lifesaver. Which of the seven abundance tools might you need to exercise a little in this moment? If you are clear on what it is you want to bring into your life and have done your inner and outer work to bring it in, check to see you've flexed your other abundance-creating muscles adequately.

Are you good at receiving and have you looked deeply at your Shadow material? Are you practicing your I AMs and coming from love, not fear, as often as possible? Are you paying attention to the synchronicity in your life that is serving as a roadmap and grateful for all that you *do* have?

Here is a summary of the tools you've received from *Beep! Beep!* as a reminder of their purpose and power. Now that you are familiar with them, call on them whenever you need them.

DEEP DESIRE + WORK

THE FIRST TOOL IS GETTING crystal clear on what it is you want to call forth and then doing the work to make it happen.

Don't stop thinking about your point of attraction! Thinking of it as something planted in your soul when you arrived or something in your DNA that you are here to manifest may help you stay on track when bringing it in. Whatever it is you deeply desire to do, have, or be, lives in you for a reason. Every well-intended goal or desire is your soul's dream and mandate and within your power to bring into reality or it wouldn't be inside of you.

We did not come here to waste this incarnation. We came to learn, to love, to share our gifts, and to be authentically ourselves.

Imagine, for one moment, you one year from now. Imagine not having, being, or doing the thing it is you know you are here to have, be, or do. Or, imagine getting to the end of your life without it. How does that feel? Now imagine doing everything you can to bring it in. Yeah. That's it. Do everything you can do until it's *here*. Light a fire under your desire, think of it constantly (inner work), and do all you can do on the outside and *it will be here*, just as you imagined.

RECEIVING

RECEIVING IS WHAT HAPPENS WHEN we are strong enough to allow someone else to do something for us.

Learn to be so good at receiving that you find yourself showered in the benevolence of this bountiful planet that loves nothing more than to provide!

When we know that receiving isn't about taking, but about allowing, we may be more open to it.

SHADOW

IF YOU ARE ALIVE, YOU have a Shadow. That's just the gig. It's part of being human. We are all going to get hurt. We are all going to be teased at some time in our life. We are all going to feel abandoned at some point. We are all going to be disappointed, or not have every one of our needs met, or suffer a loss, or have to move a lot as a child, or be mistreated by an unkind person. Parents and guardians won't always be able to meet every one of our emotional, physical, or psychological needs, no matter how much they try or how good they are at parenting. And when people are jealous of our outgoing personality, our talent, looks, or brains, we learn to hide those natural gifts so they won't be threatened.

Therefore, we may believe things about ourselves based on things that happened to us as kids that we still think are true. Or we may believe we have to be a certain way to be liked, and being any other way is deemed unacceptable by us. *Stepping out of our role can feel like breaking the law.*

We cast certain traits into our Shadow because our parents, schools, places of worship, or society as a whole deemed them inappropriate. It's as if we take those traits, throw them into a dark dungeon, and forget about them. By doing so, we also forget that they may have something to teach us, may have some gold hidden inside of them.

We may be afraid to look into our Shadow, remembering that we put those unloved personal traits away for a good reason. But those traits not only fail to disappear when ignored, they grow. And they show up in the most exaggerated, inappropriate ways if suppressed. Better to bring them out, acknowledge their presence, polish them, and utilize their good sides.

But you know what? When you bring your Shadow traits out into the light, heal them, and use the positive sides of those characteristics, you will find them to be your greatest assets.

Make friends with your Shadow. It's not your enemy. It's your teacher.

I AM

YOUR I AM STATEMENTS ARE declarations to the world of who you think you are. Everything you put after I AM is a declarative statement that not only your unconscious mind will believe, everyone else will too. Choose wisely. The attributes and adjectives you put after I AM will come in search of you and stay with you long after you have spoken them.

People treat you as you treat yourself, and you show people how you think you deserve to be treated. You actually *teach* them how to treat you. You do this with the I AMs you state, silently and out loud, consciously and unconsciously. Your I AMs telegraph how you feel about yourself to the world.

Your I AM-ness, your very being, is unique in the history of place and time. Remembering your I AM statements and expressing them with intention is a game-changer.

LOVE VERSUS FEAR

Sure, fear serves a purpose. Pay attention to it when it shows up. It wants to protect you. It is sometimes legitimate and should be heeded. But when making most of your life decisions, let love be your guide. What is the loving thing to do for yourself, for others, for the highest good? You can simply ask, "Am I coming from love or fear right now?" and get an intuitive answer very quickly.

There is no dress rehearsal for your life and your dreams, no parallel Universe running alongside this one, as far as I know, where we can try Option A and Option B in a specific instance to see what the best outcome will be. We can only make as many of our choices, as often as possible, from our best and highest self. Another name for that best and highest self is "love."

We can't be in a place of fear and love at the same time.

Choose love. Love is a helluva lot more fun.

SYNCHRONICITY

Synchronicity is what happens when we and the Universe are dancing together.

Synchronicity is what shows up in signs, songs, words we read, people showing up at just the right time, and messages we receive that show us that we are on track at that very moment in ways that defy all odds. It's the Universe's way of catching our attention. We feel supported and guided when synchronicity shows up and when we pay attention to it. You increase the probability of it happening when you pay attention to the signs synchronicity brings you: The praying mantis on your gate, the hummingbird, dragonflies, and butterflies that visit you in your yard, and the recurring number might all be little messengers for you.

Synchronicity is included as one of the abundance tools for two reasons. One is that, as you step into receiving more of what you want that may be new for you, it's nice to get signs from the Universe that you are on track and supported. Think of instances of synchronicity as signposts telling you that you are going in the right direction. They are also helpful if we are a little unsure of exactly what it is we desire. For example, if you know your current career is not a good match, that you want to leave and want "more" but aren't sure what is a good fit, you can ask the Universe for signs that point you in the right direction.

Synchronicity is the flashlight the Universe hands us when we are traveling on a road in the dark at just the moment when we think, "I can't see where I am going."

GRACE AND GRATITUDE

IF SYNCHRONICITY IS THE FLASHLIGHT the Universe hands us just when we think, "I can't see where I am going," grace is the flashlight it hands us before we noticed we needed one. Grace provides for us just because that's the generous and loving thing to do.

Grace is like that.

There is no other you. No one else has your one precious life. It's yours by fate, by circumstance, by the grace of the Universe, or whatever you want to call it. But it's yours. Only yours. We can't really get this party started without you because your unique thread is a very necessary part of the tapestry. Gratitude, the second part of this tool, is being appreciative for that opportunity and for all the gifts along the way, including the ones "wrapped in sandpaper."

Early one morning, I walked out of my bedroom and into the yard to go to the meditation chair in the garden when I heard and felt a *whoosh* by my head. At first, I wasn't sure what it was. "Was that a bird?" I wondered. That made me think there must be a bird's nest nearby. Whatever it was seemed to originate from a candleholder hanging from the eaves in the patio rafters high above my head. Without peeking in and disturbing anything, I held my phone camera high above my head over the candleholder and pointed it downward, not knowing what it might capture.

When I looked at the photo, sure enough, there were five small light blue eggs and the bird that had flown by was the mama to those eggs.

How marvelous to have something so precious and unexpected within a few steps from my door! Discovering the nest felt like a call to slow down. How many things are ready to birth right in front of us? How much beauty is hidden just out of view but available if we search a little bit?

There is so much hope, promise, synchronicity, birth and rebirth, peace, quiet, and joy surrounding us at any given moment. And if we don't see it on the outside because of where we are standing, *we can always turn inward and find it there.*

How incredible is it that we find ourselves in human form at this one, precious moment! How rare an opportunity to come exactly as the "we" we're made to be, and how exquisite!

Slow down and see what's right in front of you, as often as you can.

That's what grace would have us do.

* * *

THIS BOOK AND THE SEVEN tools it provides have the power to change your life. Participants in my Abundance Circles and I saw the manifestation of desires called in that had felt nearly impossible to attract. On a regular basis, in sometimes miraculous fashion, people had in their lives, the very thing that said they wanted to attract.

One Abundance Circle client wanted to quit his highly lucrative but unsatisfying investment job to coach children and travel with his wife and kids, but was worried about the resulting loss of income. Without the job, there would be no travel. But his job was distasteful to him and coaching and travel were his passion. He took the leap, saying that the Love Versus Fear tool and support from his Abundance Circle group gave him the courage to do so. He has since taken vacations all over the world with his family and does so from a stream of income that was unknown at the time he made the leap and would have remained unknown had he not taken it.

The vast majority of people who said they wanted to attract a committed relationship after years of dating unsuitable matches or no one at all actually met the person they would eventually marry during the four months the circles gathered! It was so exciting and breathtakingly beautiful to watch them go from gleeful excitement to a bit of guarded caution: "Is this too good to be true?!" to "I think he is The One!" and moving in together or getting married some time later. I even officiated one such wedding! They told me it would be only fitting.

The same was true when financial abundance was the goal. Participants' businesses grew or money came from unexpected sources. Some participants left jobs they'd been miserable in for years but had been too nervous to leave until they got the courage and strength to do so from their Abundance Circles experience, only to find a better one that paid more and where they were happy. Several who were out of work when they joined a circle found great careers while still in the circle, like the single mother mentioned earlier in the book. People with businesses got more clients or felt more confident in raising their rates, or both. Writers published their manuscripts. Actors booked auditions.

Some credited the Love Versus Fear tool for their ability to shift their money story. Others said they had to learn to receive in life and that made a difference. For others, the I AM tool made them more confident to go after what they wanted. And some felt that applying the Deep Desire + Work tool made the biggest shifts in their lives.

But the secret sauce is applying *all* the tools. Each one of them is precious as a diamond. Together they are an alchemical elixir for calling in that which your heart deeply desires. And because the things our heart most deeply desires are usually love and the financial freedom to do the things closest to our hearts, it's powerful to realize that our personal energy is *the* magnet that attracts or repels those things.

Love and its subcategories (finding our soulmate, marriage, peace) and money (prosperity, abundance, financial freedom, not being stuck in a job we hate, being able to travel and engage in hobbies) are the two main areas Abundance Circle participants come to me to address. Money and love are just energy. That's all! And love is a high-frequency energy. Who doesn't want to luxuriate in that?!

I know how deeply you want what your heart so desires. I know how soul-crushing it is to want it so desperately and for so long, only for it to remain heartbreakingly out of reach for years. Being mindful of my own thoughts and energy with regard to my desire and these tools shifted everything. These tools have changed my life. My story shifted from "I don't get to have" to "Who am I to play so small?" I do more good, effect more change, and am happier when I embody my full and authentic self. That's true for all of us.

Study these seven tools in order and spend a fair amount on each one. We spend two weeks between sessions in the Abundance

Circles, and that seems the perfect amount of time for the tool to fully marinate. We are talking slow-cooker simmer here, not a flash fry. When one tool feels complete or fully integrated, step into the next one as you would slip into a warm, full bubble bath. Slide in. Submerge yourself in each new tool as you would submerge yourself in bathwater, letting it carry and calm you. With your mind clear and body relaxed, let the tool surround you, the way it feels when you sink deep into a tub.

Then, while studying each tool, do your due diligence. Be on the lookout for whatever tool you are on at the time to show up in your life. Then see how you can practice it or put it use.

The clearer we get from doing this inner work and healing, the more it frees things up to come to us at an accelerated rate. Fasten your seatbelt! You may not be used to the speed, or to having what you ask for actually showing up! The more you allow things to come in with love, versus being afraid and constricting your life from fear, the easier it gets, and the more fun life becomes!

If you were not meant to fulfill the dream you carry in your heart, it would not have been placed there. You now have the tools to bring that dream into your reality.

I—and the rest of the world—cannot wait to see what that dream of yours looks like manifested in the world. We are waiting for it with great anticipation and excitement!

Look out, world!

This is your moment now.

Beep! Beep, world! Hot stuff comin' through.

The End

ACKNOWLEDGMENTS

I WOULD LIKE TO ACKNOWLEDGE and give special thanks to all my Abundance Circle participants; past, present and future, who by dreaming boldly and believing in the power of their visions, manifested the life they dreamt of and inspired this book. It was an honor sitting together with you in Circles and witnessing both your vulnerability and glee when what you deeply desired to have show up in your life, SHOWED UP IN YOUR LIFE! So proud of you and happy for you! I love you, Abundance Angels!

Thank you to Kristina Paider who was my rock, my reader, my cheerleader. I could not, would not, have been able to complete this book without you. So deeply grateful to and for you, dear soul.

Thank you too for the friends who continually checked in with me and the process of this book over the long period it took to complete it. Your love, compassion and support meant the world to me. It always came at the perfect time.

Thank you too Spirit Team. You know who you are.

ABOUT THE AUTHOR

CATHERINE DEMONTE IS A PSYCHOTHERAPIST IN PRIVATE practice for over 25 years, and creator of the "Abundance Circles," which have helped countless participants manifest their deepest desires: long-term partners, extraordinary financial shifts, or long-dreamed about projects finally brought to life. She takes a stand on helping people become their best and highest self and to live their fullest, most authentic, joyous lives.

Catherine is a recognized relationship expert, abundance-creator and positivity spreader. She lives in California with her beloved of thirty-five years and has two sons. *Beep! Beep! Get Out of My Way! Seven Tools for Living Your Unstoppable Life* is her first book.

Connect with Catherine at http://www.catherinedemonte.com/index.html

CPSIA information can be obtained
at www.ICGtesting.com
Printed in the USA
FSHW020710190619
59196FS